Under the Crown

51 Stories of Courage, Determination
and the American Spirit

"Courage doesn't always roar. Sometimes courage is the quiet voice at the end of the day saying. 'I will try again tomorrow.'"

– Mary Anne Radmacher-Hershey

Under the Crown

51 Stories of Courage, Determination and the American Spirit

Katie Harman
Miss America 2002

with

The 2001 Miss America Contestants

Milestone Books

Distributed by

Seattle, Washington

Dedication

To Victor J. Saracine
and all the heroes and families of
September 11, 2001.

Contents

Acknowledgments xiii
Foreword xv
Introduction xvii
Miss Alabama 2001 1
Miss Alaska 2001 5
Miss Arizona 2001 9
Miss Arkansas 2001 13
Miss California 2001 17
Miss Colorado 2001 19
Miss Connecticut 2001 23
Miss Delaware 2001 27
Miss Florida 2001 31
Miss Georgia 2001 35
Miss Hawaii 2001 39
Miss Idaho 2001 43
Miss Illinois 2001 47
Miss Indiana 2001 51
Miss Iowa 2001 55
Miss Kansas 2001 59
Miss Kentucky 2001 63
Miss Louisiana 2001 67
Miss Maine 2001 69
Miss Maryland 2001 73
Miss Massachusetts 2001 77
Miss Michigan 79
Miss Minnesota 2001 83
Miss Mississippi 2001 87

Miss Missouri 2001 91
Miss Montana 2001 95
Miss Nebraska 2001 99
Miss Nevada 2001. 103
Miss New Hampshire 2001 107
Miss New Jersey 2001 111
Miss New Mexico 2001. 115
Miss New York 2001 119
Miss North Carolina 2001 123
Miss North Dakota 2001 127
Miss Ohio 2001 131
Miss Oklahoma 2001 135
Miss Oregon 2001. 139
Miss Pennsylvania 2001 143
Miss Rhode Island 2001 147
Miss South Carolina 2001 151
Miss South Dakota 2001 155
Miss Tennessee 2001 159
Miss Texas 2001 163
Miss Utah 2001 167
Miss Vermont 2001 171
Miss Virginia 2001 175
Miss Washington 2001 179
Miss Washington D.C. 2001 183
Miss West Virginia 2001 187
Miss Wisconsin 2001 191
Miss Wyoming 2001 195

Acknowledgments

To all of you who have touched our lives so lovingly —
who have inspired us
to reach higher and farther than we ever imagined,
and who encouraged us to remain steadfast and involved,
our deepest gratitude.
  – The Contestants of
  Miss America 2001

George F. Bauer III

Foreword

You may already know that the Miss America Organization is the largest provider of scholarships for young women in the world. And, you probably know that these dedicated young women who compete for the coveted Miss America title, and the thousands of volunteers around the country, donate more than 500,000 hours each year to make it one of the largest service organizations in the country. The following stories demonstrate the shared spirit of the young ladies who participated in the Miss America experience, "The Class of 2001," and they illustrate why I am so proud of them.

These young women pursue the road to excellence in order to help others. They are inspirational speakers and role models. They are committed to honing their skills, enabling them to positively influence and change the lives of others. Each of these caring young ladies strives to be the best she can be — enhancing and illuminating her intelligence through education.

On September 11, 2001, a new concept of thinking was tragically forced upon all of us.

On that terrible day that shook the very soul of our nation, we all experienced roller-coaster-like feelings running from numbness to overwhelming emotions, to fear and love, to reaching out and introspection. Out of that emotional turbulence was born a powerful bonding, strength given and received, and a foreshadowing of what was to come. From the depth of their spiritual strength, there emerged for these women a clear picture of their beliefs and what they stood for.

On September 13th, after long and careful thought, after examining pros and cons and the rippling effects that would be created — big or small — they decided to go on with the competition. Out of respect for a grieving nation, the show was clad in a more inspirational mood, and even helped raise money for the September 11 Fund.

With their decision to stand firm, the Miss America contestants proved that they would not be intimidated, and led their own charge in America's fight against terrorism.

There was no empty rhetoric that day — the "walk matched the talk." In those terrifying moments of uncertainty, this group representing America's future, offered its own brand of inspirational guidelines for all of us. These young women exemplified leadership skills, strength of character and spirit. This book is an example of what they do ... *they touch lives!*

In closing, I would like to recognize our volunteers, staff and all those involved with the Miss America 2001 competition. They, too, were away from their homes and families, but firmly held their ground and supported our contestants.

We are so proud to be working with these young women. Here are their special insights.

> – George F. Bauer III
> Interim President
> Chief Executive Officer
> The Miss America Organization

Photography by Gideon Lewin

Introduction
by
Katie Harman
Miss America 2002

Empty metal folding chairs littered one end of an enormous ballroom tucked within Atlantic City's historic Boardwalk Hall, soon to be occupied by fifty-one young women who had arrived in the city the day before with dreams of becoming the next Miss America. The chairs were not arranged in neat rows, rather strewn in a fashion that seemed to lack purpose or definition. Despite their disarray, they faced two large television sets perched on the edge of the stage; the televisions revealing horrifying images of a tragedy maliciously calculated to undermine the spirit of America.

At approximately noon on September 11, 2001, the contestants of the 82nd Miss America Competition filed into the ballroom with tear-streaked faces and heavy hearts having learned that morning of the acts of terrorism that had taken place in our country. Each wrestled in her spirit with the sudden shift of dynamics. At that moment, she was a grieving American, which seemed far removed from being simply the contender for the title of Miss America 2002. Amidst fear, sorrow, and bewilderment swirled doubt as to the purpose of her presence at the competition during such a time. The sparkle of the crown was suddenly concealed behind a shadow of grief that enveloped the nation.

Slowly, each young woman settled into one of the folding chairs, slightly adjusting its position, and moving closer to the "sister" at her side. Three hours later the chairs once again stood empty and unorganized at all angles.

When the morning sun streamed through the ballroom's large bay windows on September 12th, the chairs were no longer scattered. Instead, each young woman had positioned her respective chair forming a fifty-one-seat circle. What was once chaos and despair, became purpose and determination. The chairs became platforms for the contestants to express their opinions about the relevance of the 2001 Miss America Competition. Questions darted from woman to woman in an attempt to make a sound, sensitive and common decision whether the competition should continue.

Would a telecast of this nature be suitable for a grieving nation? Were they as individuals and as a class prepared to face the needs of American citizens? Did the country still need a Miss America? In a two-to-one vote, the contestants resolved that terrorists would not bring down the Miss America Organization — a time-honored program committed to outfitting goal-driven young women with the scholarship dollars and skills necessary to inspire a people in need. Indeed, the American people needed a Miss America.

I recall feeling as empty and scattered as those metal folding chairs when I first heard the news of the cowardly terrorist attacks on the the World Trade Center, the Pentagon and the downed plane in Pennsylvania — not quite knowing what my role was at that time or in which direction I should go. When placed within the circle of my Class of 2001 sisters, however, I drew strength from the power of our collective order, gaining purpose. Our decision to proceed motivated me to dig deeper into my perspective of the job of Miss America and uncover the true value of its opportunities. I felt strongly that my responsibility as a member of the Miss America Organization — whether returning to my home state as Miss Oregon 2001, or being selected to serve my country as Miss America 2002 — entailed imparting the same sense of hope and healing that my sisters had instilled in me, in others.

Today, when I look at the crown that was placed atop my head on September 22, 2001, I am moved by its likeness to the circle formed by our quest for purpose at that meeting. Although the crown was awarded to me that night, it truly also belongs to the fifty courageous young women who stood beside me to deliver a message of hope to the nation. Just as the image of the crown relies on the unity of its stones, so does the strength of a nation on the resolve of its citizens … citizens like the contestants of the 82nd Miss America Competition. I am honored to have served our communities, our states and our nation alongside them. I am also reminded of a powerful poem written by Louisa May Alcott:

> *I do not ask for any crown*
> *But that which all may win.*
> *Not try to conquer any world*
> *Except the one within.*

Under our crown you will find fifty-one stories documenting the quest of the Class of 2001 to impart hope and healing during a year of service like no other. My prayer is that those who read our stories feel encouraged also to live with resolve during this time in our nation's history. May we never forget the power of a common goal.

– Katie Harman
Miss America 2002

Miss Alabama 2001

Kelly Jones

Bloom Where You're Planted

*D*etermination rises from desperation, pride and fear and hope from doom; I have both witnessed and experienced it. September 11 led the vast majority of Americans into a range of new emotions and self inspection. We wanted to cry; we wanted to throw up our hands in disbelief; we wanted to dig through the rubble for an explanation; we wanted a face on whom we could take revenge. Most Americans experienced these feelings for the first time. These emotions, while on a much larger scale, were all too familiar to me. Seeing the World Trade Center towers smoldering and crumbling to the disbelief of all those around me, left me with the same empty feeling I had in my stomach much earlier as I lay in the intensive care unit of a hospital suffering from toxic shock syndrome, and not knowing if I would live to fight another day.

Being in Atlantic City on September 11 was a unique and challenging time. Competing in the Miss America pageant on the

1

heels of this national tragedy was the last thing on all of the contestants' minds. Most of us were thousands of miles away from home and were concerned about what our own families were facing. My family had become strong before this disaster happened through challenges of a different kind.

Knowing we had overcome adversity earlier in the year, I realized that we could be strong during a time of great challenge in our nation. I have never been a quitter. My mother taught me at an early age to "Bloom where I was planted." Over the course of many years, I have applied this bit of wisdom to persevere despite an overwhelming desire in some cases to take the easier road. Through my time as Miss Alabama, I was able to grow and blossom and encourage everyone to do the same.

I knew that it was my mission as a state titleholder to encourage the people I met to accept everyone despite the differences that we may all have. Through the experience on January 24, 2001 and September 11, 2001 at the Miss America pageant, I have been able to flourish and grow as a person. Emerging from danger and instead of throwing in the towel, I began to learn that life's obstacles make us better people, and offer us new opportunities to relate with people from all different walks of life.

I began competing in the Miss America system as a way to fund my college education and with the belief that I would gain a new sense of confidence and self-esteem. I never imagined that my years of participating would culminate in competing in the Miss America pageant. I first became involved in 1997 and adopted the *Boys and Girls Club* for my community service outlet. I began working with youth to encourage them to become positive role models. At the time in the teens' lives when peer pressure is so prevalent, it is imperative that we educate these young men and women on the importance of making wise decisions. Along the way, I was able to establish wonderful relationships with many young people. Through these friendships I was able to see my own life come full circle.

I believe that life is like a chain reaction. I think a cycle of it started for me when I spent eight days in the hospital overcoming the toxic shock aliment. This happened only six months before the Miss Alabama pageant. I was attending graduate school, and had been coaching thirty-four piano students. Fortunately, I had already won my local preliminary a few weeks before my illness. If I had not done that, I would have been unable to compete in a local pageant preceding that for the Miss Alabama title, and would have lost my chance to win.

When I was released from the hospital on February 1, I was weak from loss of muscle and had to embark on a concentrated program to regain my strength. Even so, I was handicapped by the loss of handfuls of my hair due to the medications I had to take which saved my life. I wore hair pieces at both the Miss Alabama and Miss America competitions. In pageants, so much emphasis is placed on physical beauty, but I learned that what truly counts is what you are on the inside.

Being in the presence of the other state titleholders on the morning of September 11, is something I will never forget, because everyone's inner beauty became so evident. We created a lasting bond between us that will never be broken. We each became a link in a chain of strength and determination that held all 51 of us together in a common purpose to instill in Americans a new sense of hope; it was our obligation and honor. It is amazing how the events in our our lives can come full circle. After being admitted to the hospital, I discovered that the daughters of both my doctors had been influenced by a peer role model program I had started. That night as the doctors were saving my life, I am sure they knew who I was.

We never know who will be the heroes in our lives. Often we already know them. I learned through my illness and my Miss America experience to treat everyone in my life as heroes. This way we can build a tower of support that no one can ever tear down.

Miss Alaska
2001

Eugenia Primis

Music Sings the Song of Life

*W*hen I was seventeen years old and a senior in high school, I was approached by a local pageant director with the idea of competing for the title of Miss Alaska. I thought, "Why not? What a wonderful opportunity to earn scholarship money for college." It sounded like a great idea. I was required to choose a platform issue, and, having studied the cello since the age of four, there was no platform as appropriate as one dealing with the importance of music in the lives of young children. I worked for the next three years in public schools, demonstrating my love of music and my dedication to the values of music education. But it was not until the traumatic events of September 11, 2001, while competing at the Miss America pageant, that I realized my platform carried a much deeper significance.

My first concern, after the shock of the news, was for my two brothers living in Manhattan. After failing to get through by phone to either of them or to my sister in Boston, I called home to Alaska. A wave of relief washed over me when my mother informed me that she had spoken to my brothers and they were safe.

My next fear was that I would not be able to get back home. Alaska is so far away. What if something else happens? What about the pageant? Who cares!

I just wanted to be home with my family. Competing for Miss America was the farthest thing from my mind. However, over the next couple of days, it became quite clear to me how important it was to show the world that we as a nation would be strong, and that we would not have our lives disrupted.

As the week continued and it was decided to go on with the Miss America pageant, I thought it might be impossible for my delegation to get out of Anchorage to be at my side.

My family however, found a way to fly the long distance despite all the chaos. Each night when I competed, I felt their presence and knew that they were cheering me on, even in the absence of so many others who had planned to come to support me.

The exhausting week finally ended, but I knew my job as Miss Alaska had taken on a new meaning entirely. I returned to my state a stronger person, realizing now more than ever, the importance of Music for a Sound Education project. A new aspect was added to my goal of making music important in a child's life. It could be a way to promote peace.

Being in Atlantic City at a time of tragedy, reminded me of the recent sorrow in my own life. The sudden death of my father came only two months before I won the title of Miss Alaska. It was a struggle for me to continue competing for Miss America, but my father always said, "if you are going to do something, make sure you do it all the way." So I kept going. I became a stronger person as a result. I know now that even out of the most tragic events, opportunities arise. And this was so of the attack on America at a cost of thousands of lives. We Americans have been reawakened to the blessings we have.

From my own training as a cellist, studying the works of the great Pablo Casals, I learned that he devoted his distinguished career to the cause of world peace. He used his fame to embark on his own personal crusade to promote peace. He once said, "Music must serve a purpose; it must be a part of something larger than itself, a part of humanity...."

I am convinced that if we incorporate music as an integral part of our everyday lives, and instill its values in our children, that someday it will, in some way, bring peace to this world. I also love the thought expressed by Gustav Holst: "Music, being identical with Heaven, isn't a thing of momentary thrills, or even hourly ones: it's a condition of eternity."

In a world of peace and love, music would be the universal language.

– Henry David Thoreau

Miss Arizona
2001

Kapri Rose

The Love for Each Other

*T*o Miss America, I took eight trunks. The first was filled entirely with shoes. My mom crammed my favorite pillow into the corner of another, and somehow my family found room in others for little love notes, reminding me to smile and practice and wear the beige bag with the beige shoes (of utmost importance, you understand). To Miss America, I took things that seemed so crucial at the time: the rhinestone sandals, the silver earrings, the raspberry lipstick.

I was just nineteen when I stepped on a plane as Miss Arizona, bound for the Miss America pageant. My heart was full of hope, huge dreams and an eye on a big prize: the desire to represent my nation. Days later, everything changed. September 11, struck the eastern seaboard, and the entire nation was stunned and confused by burning buildings and layers of smoke. The Miss America pageant passed in a blur of new patriotism and more earnest love.

The day after the pageant, I took my first trip to New York City. I had planned to go as Miss Arizona, to speak about my platform and to see the Empire State Building and the lights of Broadway, to see the city that glittered and beckoned in my dreams. I went instead as an American, to see the place where America was hurting.

On September 23rd, I stood at Ground Zero, where the debris was still smoking and crowds stood by in silent support and mourning. The only words I heard were from a young girl, who asked me "Have you seen my brother?" as she held out his picture. Tears welled in my eyes and I couldn't find the words to answer that awful question.

As I walked around the site, I found a place where I could get right up close to the debris. It was dark and the smoke was heavy and acrid. I saw hand prints left on dust-covered buildings. Light posts were covered with "Missing" signs: "Have you seen my brother? my mother? my friend?"

I was looking at what was left of the mighty World Trade Center's Twin Towers, pondering the impossibility of it all, when a man next to me started to clap, and the wordless crowd joined in. They were applauding a fireman emerging from that stack of dust to take a break. He was sobbing. To me, that fireman will always represent my nation in the way I had hoped to do: he gave help where help was needed, loved his country, and was a portrait of the land of the brave.

Coming home from the Miss America competition, I brought with me an image of a true American and a new desire to do good. But sometimes, in the weird, wild world of pageantry, doing good is the biggest challenge of all.

When I was six, I won my first crown — dance queen. Thirteen years later I got another one and it felt great! Adults aren't supposed to like crowns, I thought. But know this — crowns *are* addicting.

I won the title of Miss Arizona my first year in the Miss America system. I was motivated by the opportunity to perform on the piano, the opportunity to win funds to help with dental school, and the opportunity to promote a cause that has a tender place in my world. My cousin Ben has Down syndrome and, knowing the joy he brings to my family, I wanted to discourage abortion of Down syndrome babies and show others what I see in these people. We all seem to think that people with Down syndrome are different, and we are the barometer of "normal." But as I have worked with these people, I have come to realize that they are normal, and we are the different ones. They love unconditionally and don't judge others based on superficial things. These qualities should be our goal, our true "normal" barometer.

When the pageant system got too frustrating — when I couldn't perform my talent at the Miss America competition, because my song was already taken, when other problems that should not matter clouded my life — I found comfort in remembering that the crown comes with the power to make a difference. Because of my work on my Miss Arizona platform, I have so many new, close friends who may look a lot different than I do, but love in a way that I have never known.

Now that my year as Miss Arizona is over, I am embarking on a new journey: marriage. On July 3, 2002, I became the wife of Brant Roberts. We will live in Arizona while I pursue my dream of being an orthodontist. I will continue my work promoting disability accceptance as a spokesperson for Best Buddies International, an organization that forms one-to-one friendships between those with disabilities and those without. This program helps us all see the beauty in others, and my hope is that someday, organizations like this will not be necessary, and that one day, these friendships will form naturally.

Looking back on my year wearing the crown of Miss Arizona, I treasure the things that I will always take with me:

- The love of children with Down syndrome, whose hearts showed me how to be pure.
- The love of my family, manifested in hand-beaded evening gowns and cheers and laughter through tears.
- And the image of that fireman at Ground Zero, who gave me a testimony of the heart of a true American. He taught me, through his tears, that I can represent America for ever in my heart by carrying with me that most simple and human of devotions: love for each other.

Miss Arkansas 2001

Jessie Ward

The Land of the Free

O n June 17th, 2001 a defining moment in my life occurred. I was given the opportunity to represent the Natural State in Atlantic City for the 2001 Miss America Pageant. I had no idea that in being selected as a state titleholder, I would be a part of history, not only for my state but for the entire nation.

On the plane ride to Philadelphia I felt an incredible sense of peace. I knew at that moment, I was exactly where I was meant to be. I was determined to approach this experience with a positive attitude and complete confidence in God to lead me on the road that was right for me.

After spending the first few days in Philadelphia, I began to appreciate and understand the origin of our freedoms as Americans. I look at that time as ironic, considering that we were in the great city of Philadelphia where so much of our nation's early history was made. It was only a few days later that the values expressed so long ago at Independence Hall would be challenged by terrorists.

We arrived in Atlantic City on September 10, to begin a week of rehearsals and competition. Focused on our upcoming competitions, we had no idea how that focus would soon change.

On the morning of September 11, my state traveling companion, Elizabeth Farris, got me out of bed to prepare for costume fittings needed for the Saturday night production with the rest of the contestants. I had already met three special women — Miss Michigan, Stacey Essebaggers, Miss Hawaii, Denby Dung and Miss Oregon, soon to become Miss America 2002, Katie Harman. We stayed in the same hotel and shared the ride from our hotel to the convention center each morning and each evening after competition.

Several of us were in the dressing room when we heard about the attacks that froze us to our chairs in disbelief and horror. There was no television where we were, but one of the contestants found a radio under a table and we plugged into the news the entire nation was hearing. We sat in dead silence as Tom Brokaw reported the details of the tragedy in New york and at the Pentagon. We listened as this veteran newscaster who had reported devastation, disaster and death around the world for many years, fell silent in a moment of intense emotion and fear. I remember him repeating, "There are truly no words to describe what is happening."

Each contestant dealt with the tragedy in her own way. However, as we sat in that dressing room consoling and supporting each other, the focal point of competing for the crown of Miss America quickly faded.

There we sat, 51 young women representing the great states of our great nation, role models for thousands of young women, epitomizing the rights and freedoms that Americans celebrate — helpless and afraid. After returning to my room, several messages were waiting for me. My family, friends and supporters were worried sick. I spent lots of time on the phone assuring everyone that we were fine. My mother was quick to point out a fact I had not taken the time to realize: we were only two hours away from the the the World Trade Center.

My sister had been at school that day, and her classmates had convinced her that I was probably in the Twin Towers, and she would never see me again.

My dad arrived at her school to pick her up for a dentist appointment, and in tears, she believed he was coming to get her to tell her that I had been killed in the attacks. For a short while, our household was turned upside down. Yet, my family was adamant that if the pageant was to go on, they would be there. Many of the delegation from Arkansas had decided not to attend the event. I was so glad to see familiar family faces supporting me, but I was equally showered with support from those who were there in thought only.

When we met with the CEO of the Miss America Organization, to decide whether or not to go on with the pageant, I voted to continue. I am just a stubborn Southern girl who believes in her freedoms and refuses to allow terrorists to limit her right to celebrate one of the greatest traditions in American history.

My mind was made up when we were told that the focus of the show would be changed to a tribute to America and to those who lost so much during the events in New York and Washington D.C. It was the right decision. As a nation, we were ready for something lighter and uplifting on our televisions.

After returning to Arkansas to serve my state, I reflected on this time with great pride and humility. I was honored to be a part of the 2001 class of contestants, but I was even prouder to have represented the rights and freedoms that we celebrate as Americans and as women in a changing and sometimes unstable world.

The Miss America Organization has served as a cornerstone for women for many years. We have been through many changes and have always kept the welfare of our nation in mind. Once again we have risen to the occasion in the face of adversity. I am proud to be a part of a group of women who still believes we truly live in the land of the free and the home of the brave.

Miss California 2001

Stephanie Baldwin

Carrying the Message

I have often thought that my generation has nothing that connects and brings us all together. I believe we don't have a strong sense of responsibility or loyalty to our country and fellow Americans. This lack was apparent in my own interactions with older generations. Now, I can share the pain of witnessing on film such terrible events as the attack on Pearl Harbor, the assassination of President Kennedy, World War II, and the Great Depression. Now I, too, as Miss California, have felt penetrating fear and loss.

The events of September 11, have affected me as a person more than me as Miss California. I am more aware of how I live my life and the choices I make. I do, however, see myself as a leader and a role model to all of those I have served this year. I have been asked to sing patriotic songs more often, and I have felt blessed to have the opportunity to express my love and appreciation for my country.

Those who serve and protect us all, whether on the streets of my home town of Placentia, California or in the deserts of a land remote to us, deserve our utmost respect and gratitude. I have found that singing songs that praise America at each event — from the groundbreaking of the Orange County Fire Department Training Center to veteran hospitals here and there, to the USO in San Diego — has been therapeutic for me, and I think for those who listened to my voice. I am the first to stand proudly when the flag goes by, or to request others to "please stand for our national anthem." Maybe more boldly.

I also led by flying all over the world. I flew home from Atlantic City on September 23rd, and less than a month later, I was on my way to France. I was given the option to forego my international trips this year, because of the potential threat from terrorists, but I was determined not to let caution or fear influence my life. That was part of the decision of the women of the Miss America Class of 2001.

We decided that we must represent the best America can be everywhere we went. In the person of each one of us resides the dedication to our country to stand against tyranny, against the enemies of freedom. We were the living symbols of liberty.

I carried that message to my fellow Americans and to people all over the world. To France, Grand Cayman, Singapore, Taipei, Hong Kong and Tokyo. I represented the Stars and Stripes.

Personally, I attempt to show my love and appreciation to all of my family, friends and neighbors every day. This is by no means a perfected task, but I try to show my loved ones how important, special and loved they are.

We all are.

Miss Colorado 2001

Kelly Mckee

A Dream Come True

I always felt that it was my destiny to be in the Miss America pageant. My parents both grew up near Atlantic City, New Jersey, where the event is held every year. It was a tradition in our family to watch the pageant on television. Mom and Dad were both in the pageant during the 1960s. She was part of the show's entertainment as an Atlantic City High School baton twirler, and he had accepted a dare to try out as an escort for the evening gown portion of the show. He made it. So every year I watched the show convinced that one day I would be on that stage.

As a first year competitor in the Miss Colorado pageant, I experienced a small dose of the shock that was to be magnified for me a thousand times at the Miss America pageant in Atlantic City when I learned about the attack on the Twin Towers in New York. The event that frightened the competitors of the Miss Colorado pageant occurred on the evening of the preliminary competitions held in La Junta, a small town in the southeastern part of the state.

I was sitting in a hotel room with several other girls when there was an urgent rapping on the door. A frantic state board member ordered us to grab our shoes and follow her to a shelter where we would be safe from a tornado spotted five miles away from us and heading in our direction.

I grabbed my cell phone to call my family, and felt panicky when I had trouble getting a dial tone. Outside it was pouring rain and lightning flashed through the sky. Some girls worried about leaving behind their gowns and jewelry, and I remember thinking how foolish of them.

Luckily, the tornado lifted before it reached our hotel. By the following day, the threat of being hit by a tornado was just a funny story, and the competition at hand was back on my mind. I didn't win that year and was terribly crushed. But the following year I was lucky enough to win my first local competition, and consequently, the title of Miss Colorado 2001. My dream had come true. I could not wait for the Miss America pageant. My whole life was centered on the opportunity to compete for the job of Miss America. And not just for the scholarship money. I had another agenda. My platform issue was Adoption, because I was adopted. I wanted to share my personal story and ideas about adoption with a national audience. I have been searching for my biological mother for the past seven years, and I thought that just maybe she would be watching the Miss America telecast, and somehow I might unite with her.

I always dread getting on airplanes, but I climbed aboard my flight to Miss America on September 7, pleased to make it in one piece. All of us girls spent the first few days in Philadelphia getting to know each other, and then we took a train to Atlantic City on September 10th.

September 11, was to be our first real day of rehearsals. That morning, I did not have to be at the convention center until 10:00 a.m. and I turned on the television at 9:30, only to watch in horror the vicious terrorist attack on our country. I remember thinking, "Is this really as big of a deal as I think it is?"

My traveling companion whisked me out the door and into the car that would take us to the convention center. The faces of the three other contestants already seated in the car, mirrored my shock at what we had seen on television. Pageant officials tried to start our first day of rehearsals as if nothing had happened, but none of us could seem to focus on the work at hand. We wanted to know what was going on in New York and Washington D.C., and hear the updates as they came in. Finally the CEO of Miss America stopped our practice, and we gathered around a radio to listen to the events of that terrible day.

Suddenly, nothing mattered; not even the lifelong dream of being Miss America. I remember thinking of how selfish my prayers had been. Here, I had been beseeching God to help me to do well in the competition, while so many others would have far more important prayers than mine — most importantly that their loved ones would be found alive in all the wreckage.

It was ironic to be participating in the Miss America pageant while our country was being attacked. How could the highlight of my life be happening at exactly the same time as one of our nation's worst nightmares?

It was decided among all of the girls that we should vote whether or not to go on with the pageant. When it came time for me to vote, I admit I was quite uncertain. All of us had discussed what to do.

I said that I couldn't think of anything more courageous to do, than to put aside our dreams and head back home to rally with our states. The purpose of the Miss America pageant had always been to prove that the event is more than just a beauty contest in which women would do anything to win. I felt that September 11 was the perfect opportunity to prove that we are not beauty queens, but that we are strong women with a job to do — to support and represent our state and our nation with pride and courage.

The vote to continue with the pageant carried. I did come to realize that our nation always needs a Miss America as she represents the best in all of our women. No matter who won, she would take on the responsibility of helping our nation, and be a true inspiration to emulate for every girl.

I thought that I would be devastated about not being chosen Miss America, but I was not. I was encouraged and uplifted by my 50 new sisters to do a better job as Miss Colorado. Katie Harman, our Miss America, could not do it all on her own. Each of us had a role to play of being strong, steady and unafraid role models of courage that would inspire others. I was positively charged with patriotism and I headed home knowing that I was ready to work.

One of my appearances was with Matthew Dahl, he is the son of one of the pilots killed on September 11. He turned his grief into a passion to prove to Coloradans that life goes on and we must not take one second of it for granted.

I did not take one day as Miss Colorado for granted. I was honored to be chosen to represent my state during a time when leaders and heroes can make a difference. I hope that my year as Miss Colorado made those who chose me proud that I was able to honor a heritage of responsibility and courage. As Helen Keller wrote: "Alone we can do so little; together we can do so much."

Miss Connecticut 2001

Marissa Perez

Renewed Faith

A year of renewed faith is the best way to describe my year as Miss Connecticut. It was full of many tests, and was significant because it allowed me to become a stronger person and compete in the Miss America program. By so doing, I was able to promote my platform of *Alcohol Abuse Prevention through Education* program.

I dealt with my father's alcoholism as a child, and was the scapegoat in my family for the turbulence caused by his drinking. I internalized my feelings and isolated myself from everyone, including in the classroom. I skipped lunch, because I was nauseous and was belittled by my teacher who would empty my disorganized desk in front of the class.

"Get down and clean it up," she ordered, as the others laughed. When one teacher told me that I would never make it through middle school, my fears and disorganization increased. My self-esteem grew weaker. I had no friends and could concentrate only on the constant arguing, quarreling and yelling that jarred our home at night. I couldn't talk to anyone but my diary, in which I wrote, "I hate my father and don't understand why he is making my sister, mom and me suffer." I cried myself to sleep every night.

In seventh grade, Sue Walbert, a social worker, came to our classroom and began talking to us about the effects of alcoholism on the family, how each member is influenced and spoke about the importance of getting help. I related to everything she said and everything came together for me. All of the yelling, arguing and abuse in our family were the results of my father's alcoholism. She encouraged us to come to her in confidence if any of us was facing these problems.

I started seeing Sue every day, and revealed to her my inner fears. Slowly, but surely she helped my family receive the assistance we needed. It took a lot of persistence and determination but we got through it. For years things got better, but then became worse again.

My mom never lost hope because she always put her faith in God first, and tried to instill it in us. I prayed every night, asking God to protect us, to make us stronger and allow my father to recover. I feared many things, but mostly, I feared suffering for the rest of my life. Although I received counseling, I still lacked a lot of self-confidence and knew I had do something about it.

Then I discovered the Miss America program, which encouraged contestants to promote a platform and perform a talent. I knew that despite all of the adversity I had faced, it would help me to guide others. I also knew how much I loved to sing, and that the Miss America program provided that opportunity.

I competed for Miss Connecticut five years in a row. The first year I didn't make it to the top five because my confidence level was so low. I was still quite shy, sang a country song in a long-sleeved, white lace country dress, wore red cowboy boots and a red cowboy hat. In my third year in competition, I met my fiance, Miguel, who encouraged me to compete until I won. He believed in me, and admired the fact that I wanted to win the title so I could promote the Alcohol Abuse Prevention program. As a teacher, he understood the importance of the program, for many of his students were affected by alcoholism. Finally, at the fifth competition, I was up, I sang Linda Eder's *This Time Around,* a song about accomplishing personal goals no matter what the odds. I won!

Becoming Miss Connecticut gave me the opportunity to share my own experiences with alcohol abuse with others. Schools have welcomed me; I wrote and produced a documentary entitled, *It's Not Your Fault,* focusing on the effects of alcoholism in the family. I went to the Betty Ford Center to learn more about alcohol abuse in the family and researched the recovery process.

When I competed at the Miss America pageant, the September 11 tragedy occurred. It was so easy to feel anger and hate, but growing up in a environment of faith, I knew that was the wrong thing to do. I was afraid to fall asleep, but I prayed. I took out my *Daily Bread* book — a book of faith filled with inspirational verses. As my eyes watered up that night and my heart beat rapidly, I opened it to the first page, hoping God would speak to me. He did. The lesson came to me through a story of a woman during World War II. She had been scared about the war, until she realized that God was at her side protecting and guiding her.

After reading that story, I was no longer afraid. I realized that what occurred in our country was an evil act, but prayer and faith made a difference for me. Tragedies will affect me, but they will also make me stronger as I continue growing in faith.

Miss Delaware 2001

Erin Leigh Cooper

A Wake Up Call

*I*t was supposed to be the most exciting time of my life. It was the time I had lived and relived in my mind every night I went to bed. Going to Atlantic City and participating in the Miss America Pageant was my dream come true.

What a cataclysmic collision of emotions struck me September 11, 2001 as I was running on the treadmill at the Hilton Hotel, watching the television set in front of me and preparing for a long day of rehearsal. I saw the first and the second plane crash into the World Trade Center. As the walls of these big buildings came tumbling down in a cloud of debris, I was thunderstruck in disbelief, vulnerable and scared. I had been to the World Trade Center.

This was something real; this was something close. It was not something I read about in the newspaper, or watched on television — something about a place or a people I didn't know. My college roommate walked past the Trade Center every day on her way to law school. A boy who graduated ahead of me in school worked in the Trade Center (and died there — I would find out later). My uncle is an American Airlines pilot who flies out of Boston. Could he have been on that plane? An enormous flood of sadness rushed through me!

All of the contestants gathered, numb for the most part, and discussed what we should do. It was decided that we would vote on whether to go forward with the pageant or not. Truthfully, I voted not to continue. I thought that it was a frivolous, superfluous activity in the midst of a monstrous tragedy and the pain that followed in its wake.

However, I was in the minority, and we did proceed. I must say that I understood the majority's point of view that we should not show fear, and to be brave. Honestly, I just wanted to go home and feel safe — to try to sort out the events and to understand what was happening. Instead of having the most wonderful time of my life, the event became a tedious affair for me.

How did September 11 change me?

I come from a family with a strong military background. Both of my grandfathers were career officers serving in World War II. My father, who passed away when I was fourteen, was in the Navy during the Vietnam era. My stepfather was an Air Force pilot during the Vietnam conflict. All of my life I have heard stories of their experiences, but I never really listened. I never really understood. I never really cared. This single day, September 11, gave meaning to all their experiences. How unfortunate that it took a monumental tragedy to wake me up. And how fortunate that my year as Miss Delaware gave me the opportunity to do something positive with my new awareness.

Miss Delaware is the official state hostess and is present at many state affairs. This year the events were strongly service related and more patriotic in tenor. I choreographed dances to several patriotic songs along with others. I attended many more civic events. Above all, my heart was touched by a decision made by schoolboys and girls that I will never forget.

In November, I was visiting Brandywine Springs Elementary School, where I learned that the children in first grade through sixth were saving money for their playground. However, after

September 11, they voted unanimously to donate their playground fund to the New York City firefighters and police.

On Friday, April 19, a parade was held in Wilmington, Delaware. Marching down Main Street were children from Brandywine Springs Elementary School, fire fighters and police from New York City, along with their colleagues from the police and fire departments of Delaware.

On Saturday, April 20th, a team of New York City fire fighters and police played ice hockey against a team of Delaware fire-fighters and police. Today I can't tell you who won, but I can tell you that the money raised in that ice hockey competition was presented to the children of Brandywine Springs Elementary for their new playground.

Some time later, I was present again as the two groups of fire-fighters and police were recognized by the City of Wilmington for their service to their communities.

Out of the terror of the attack on America has come for me a greater appreciation of life and a greater appreciation for the sacrifices that are made to keep me free.

Miss Florida 2001

Kelly Nicole Gaudet

The Dream

*M*y dream of becoming Miss America started long, long ago. I don't even remember the first time I saw the pageant on television, all I know is the night that Miss America was on television was much like Superbowl Sunday at our home. My mom, sister and I were ecstatic the whole day with anticipation of what was to come that evening.

"Who do you think is going to win?" was all we could think about. Like many little girls, I had this vision of what it would be like to walk down that famous runway while Bert Parks sang *There She Is, Miss America....* Not only did I imagine walking down the runway, but I envisioned just about every little detail.

I dreamed about what my dress would look like, how my hair would be done, how it would feel looking out at the audience, and the excitement of dancing on the Miss America stage. I envisioned how it might feel to have the crown placed on my head after my name was announced, followed by *There she is ...* the new Miss America!

As I grew older, I became involved in many activities, but most of my time was spent at the dance studio. I remember when I started looking at my Miss America dream as less and less of a dream, and more and more as reality. It was then I began competing in a scholarship program for young girls called, Cinderella. A friend of my parents who frequently visited our house on weekends and was familiar with the "shows" my little sister and I put on any time there was an audience, pushed my Mom to enroll the two of us in this pageant. That was the beginning of an ongoing journey that started when I was eight years old and hasn't stopped yet.

I am not sure what it was like in other states, but in Florida, Cinderella was quite popular and highly competitive. I learned so much about myself, others and life, for that matter, through this system. The Cinderella program was much like Miss America in the sense that you competed in interview, talent and evening wear. The only difference was instead of a swimsuit competition, contestants wore sportswear. The funny thing is that it would have been fabulous if there had been a swimsuit competition at the time, because back then, I was the smallest twig around.

Cinderella was an opportunity for young girls who weren't involved in sports, like myself, to have that competitive element added in their lives. Besides that, it allowed for many to fine tune their talents, and learn to cope with the fear of facing large audiences and other scary situations. It teaches a girl from a young age on how to groom and carry herself with style and grace. Another perk for me, was that I was able to watch girls who competed in Cinderella, progress to the Miss Miami Pageant, on to Miss Florida, and eventually participate in the Miss America event.

Every year, as I grew older and watched as more and more girls who I had met through Cinderella competed on television, such as Sandy Frick, Megan Welch and Dristen Ludecke, I only became more intrigued as my aspirations to follow in their footsteps heightened. I truly grew to love the feeling while standing on a stage full of anticipation of how I would do, and who would win.

Of course every girl wants to win, and the feeling of letdown when you don't, sometimes is hard to swallow. For me, it spurred me on to get back out there and try again. One of the many lessons

I learned through competition is that you take so much more away from the experience when you don't get what you want. Had it not been for this lesson, I probably would have never made it to the Miss America stage. Finally, after years of competing in dozens of talent competitions, I became Miss Palm Beach County in 1998. My platform was focused on explaining the harmful effects of smoking to elementary school students.

That same week, my father was diagnosed with pancreatic cancer. Eight months later, after a valiant fight with the disease, we lost my fifty-four year old dad.

Not long after he died, I spoke at the Sylvester Comprehensive Cancer Center about the pain of losing a family member to cancer. That night, $60,000 were raised and I changed my platform to cancer awareness.

It's funny, after all the years of watching and waiting to compete at Miss America and all the dreaming of what it would be like, I could have never prepared myself for what it turned out to be. But I have become deeply convinced that *everything* happens for a reason, and eventually the truth reveals itself.

It was manifested in the belief of each one of the 51 contestants that God had placed her at Miss America pageant at that time for a specific purpose. All of us were convinced that we were hand picked for a unique reason. And for me, it became clear that the four years I tried to win the right to compete at Miss America was to prepare myself to become a role model for people of Florida during a time when we all needed encouragement so desperately.

Speaking to young children, teenagers, adults or senior citizens, was a clarification for me to inspire a rebirth of pride in the country we have made great by displaying our respect for individualism and the potential to do anything we set our sights on. And I am proud to be a part of it all.

Miss Georgia
2001

Emily Foster

Standing Fast

*W*hat an incredible blessing this year has been for me. I have loved every minute of being Miss Georgia. The people I've met, the stories I've heard and shared, the contacts I have made, and the smiles, hugs, and high-fives I've received, have made this year truly unforgettable. I have traveled more than 60,000 miles and made over 200 appearances throughout the state promoting my platform issue, *Connecting Character to Careers*. As Georgia Department of Education's Official Spokesperson for Character Education, I have addressed students in more than 90 schools throughout the state, encouraging them to set high academic and career goals, to believe in themselves, and to persevere against all odds to pursue their dreams.

My CCC program advocates community leaders to serve as speakers and to promote the 27 character traits of the Georgia state-mandated Character Education program. Georgia's Governor, Roy Barnes, State School Superintendent Linda

Schrenko and the Georgia Department of Education have endorsed my CCC program, and it has been implemented throughout Georgia this year.

As a pianist and vocalist, I have performed for churches and civic organizations, sharing my testimony and encouraging support from business and civic leaders within the community. I was chosen to serve on the Board of Directors for the National Museum of Patriotism, received the Habersham County Chamber of Commerce "Habersham Countian of the Year" award, and was featured in the *Georgia Voyager* magazine as one of the "Famous Women of Georgia."

Throughout my reign as Miss Georgia, I have come to appreciate many things. First, I am blessed beyond my wildest imagination, and God has a specific purpose for my life. Second, I live in the most wonderful country in the world, and as a result, have the opportunity to set my goals as high as I wish, and have all the freedoms to be able to make them come true. Third, I can make a bigger difference than I could ever fathom, if I make the decision to step outside my comfort zone and freely give to others from my heart.

The children I've met this year seemed amazed that I came from an ordinary family, and that I became involved in the Miss America organization because I needed scholarship money. I did not win the first preliminary pageants I entered, and was discouraged by many as I persisted.

One of the most important lessons that my parents and mentors taught me which I have passed on to students, is that we cannot be discouraged by failure. In a time when anti-heroes, violence, drugs, teen pregnancy, and other problems assail our students, we must stand rock solid. We need to teach our youth that inner qualities are far more important than what is on the surface.

When the terrorist attacks occurred on September 11, 2001, I knew immediately that these events would change the world as we know it and would probably affect my life as well. But I could have never predicted the magnitude of this truth. All of us participants in the Miss America Pageant realized that we were in the spotlight, and that our decision could easily be subject to envy, denial, or rejection.

We gathered in a circle for prayer each day with priests, preachers, and clergymen who spoke to us and prayed with us, offering private counseling and prayer. Then, on September 14th, we observed the National Day of Prayer and were thankful for the President and for the American citizens who were positive, uplifting and hopeful. We all demonstrated great courage in confronting these issues and overcoming fear.

Being in Atlantic City during the events of September 11, 2001, and joining with 50 other girls to make the critical decision to go forward with the Miss America Pageant demonstrated exactly who we are. Like many others, we took a positive stand for our states, for our country and for the Miss America Organization. I was indescribably proud to be a part of this incredible gathering of young women who stood up for what was right, noble, and patriotic.

We were leaders for Americans, young and old alike. We knew that we must continue to be the positive role models that former Miss America contestants have been for years for the families that look up to us, and will be looking to us now, more than ever, to help set the tone for the American spirit.

I was privileged to have become close friends with Katie Harman, Miss America 2001 during my trip to Atlantic City, and even more fortunate to have had her visit my small hometown, Cornelia, Georgia — home of the Big Red Apple — twice. Everyone in Cornelia raved over Katie and was more than impressed with her poise, beauty, and sincerity. On one of her visits we decided to have a mini Miss America reunion. Visiting me and my church family and each participating in the worship service that Sunday, were Kelly Jones, Miss Alabama, Kelly Gaudet, Miss Florida, and Katie Harman, our new Miss America.

At lunch, compliments of Babyland General Hospital and Xavier Roberts, each of us was presented with our own original Cabbage Patch Kid, named after us with our matching eye and hair color, born on the day of the Miss America Pageant, and adopted on the day we were all together again. These keepsake will be treasures to always remind us of the special bond we share because of the Miss America Pageant, and our friendship that will last a lifetime.

Having graduated from the University of Georgia and having completed one year of dental school, I am returning to the Medical College of Georgia School of Dentistry in Augusta, Georgia to pursue my professional goal of becoming an orthodontist. Beyond my year of service as Miss Georgia, I plan to continue my legacy of inspiring others to join me in sharing with students the importance of character development and goal-setting.

Miss Hawaii 2001

Denby Dung

Life is a Song

"You're so ugly!" "Yeah, why don't you get some friends your own age?" "You're so fat ... you make the sidewalk crack when you walk!" My youngest sister Darah was with me during one of the most painful times of my life. "Don't listen to 'um, Den! Don't listen to 'um!" she repeated over and over, pausing only briefly to turn back and glare at them as they followed us. Although Darah was only half my size, she was my strength that day.

Because my mom was a singer and my father was a teacher, my brother and sisters and I were taught the joy of music and learning from an early age. I have had a love of music for as long as I can remember. After that hurtful day, I turned to music and began writing songs and poems more than I ever had before. I learned that although I could not find the words to voice the pain I was feeling — with music I could express my feelings without ever saying a word.

Music had played such an important role in my life that making it my profession was an easy decision. Entering a scholarship pageant, however, was not. My younger sister Dana-Li was the one who entered me in my first pageant when I was sixteen years old. Although a growth spurt and several years on the track team helped me to lose some weight, the memory of that painful time was not as easy to shed. Getting on stage in a swimsuit in front of hundreds of people was not my idea of fun, but that didn't stop my sister, who sent in my application for me. I reluctantly participated, but soon realized that I actually enjoyed it. Although I loved the experience, it was still Dana-Li who entered me in every pageant from then on"including the one that took us both to Miss Hawaii.

In March 2001, Dana entered each of us in an official preliminary of the Miss America Scholarship Program. In an unforgettable moment, I became Miss West Oahu and Dana-Li was crowned Miss Honolulu. We would be the first sisters to compete together on the Miss Hawaii stage in the fifty-three year history of the program.

We went through the entire pageant process together with twice the fun. As soon as my name was announced as the new Miss Hawaii, Dana dashed across the stage, and was the first one to hug and congratulate me. She cried out, "I'm so happy"my sister is Miss Hawaii! This is so awesome!"

The truth is, Dana entered me in pageants so that I could enjoy something that she loved so much. She believed in me long before I had the courage to believe in myself. After the pageant, she said, "I'm Miss Honolulu … together we're Miss Honolulu Hawaii." The crown was hers as much as it was mine, the moment was ours to share, and in that moment, we had both won.

With each new experience, we learn and grow, and sometimes, we are fortunate enough to meet special people who remain with us for a lifetime. On September 5, 2001, I left Hawaii eager to enjoy an incredible opportunity at Miss America. In addition to having a wonderful experience, I also made lifelong friends in the process. As soon as the contestants met for the first time, we immediately bonded by laughing, sharing, and connecting like old friends.

On September 11, we were in the Atlantic City Convention Hall getting ready for our first day of rehearsals. Suddenly, a security guard burst into our dressing room yelling that the World Trade Center had been attacked. The idea of something like that happening almost seemed impossible to believe. Then, someone found a small, old, dusty black radio, our only contact to the outside world. There were no televisions or telephones allowed in the dressing room, so we wept, prayed, and huddled close to the radio and each other, in an effort to make sense of it all.

That day, and the days following were very difficult for us all. We expressed our feelings and concerns to each other, and eventually decided that the best thing for us to do would be to move forward. Rehearsals for the pageant began. The pall that had descended on us from the attacks on the Twin Towers lifted enough for us to move ahead with new determination. When we were asked if we wanted to rehearse to a fast or slow song, we unanimously responded, "Fast song!" Minutes later, we were learning the steps for the swimsuit competition, and once again witnessed the incredible power of music.

After the show each night, all of the contestants celebrated together with family and friends. We sang, danced the hula, greeted each other, and shared the spirit of aloha with fresh flower leis. At the end of the evening, I was truly touched when my friends, with only two ukuleles and a lot of love, began singing, God Bless America. Soon, everyone in the entire room joined hands, and we were united in song and friendship.

I returned home with a rekindled passion to share my love of music with others. It has been said, "To teach … is to reach for the angels, and touch them." Being the music teacher to my little angels at Trinity Christian School was an important part of my year, as was performing as a clarinetist in the Royal Hawaiian Band. These opportunities supported the platform that I dedicated my year of service to — The Music Effect.

My music students developed an even stronger desire to learn and perform. Our spring concert was entitled, "I Could Sing of Your Love Forever" and included songs about faith, hope and love. We also included many patriotic and reflective songs in our Royal Hawaiian Band performances. With music, I have been able to deal with challenging times in my own life. Similarly, this year, many of us have found comfort and strength in music that has given us hope.

Life is a song … love is the music. All that I have encountered this year has enabled me to understand the meaning of true unconditional friendship. Now more than ever, I rejoice in my family, friends, and loved ones, and am so grateful for their love. These experiences and those who have shared so much of themselves with me have been the music that touches my heart.

Miss Idaho
2001

Christi Diane
Weible

The Journal Remembers

I watched in horror that day, like the rest of the nation, as our country, our freedoms, and our ideals came under attack. Only I watched from the twenty-third floor of my Atlantic City hotel, where I had just awakened for our first day of rehearsal at the 2001 Miss America Pageant. Fixing my hair and make-up and picking out the perfect wardrobe that morning seemed very trivial to me. I knew there must be thousands of people who had lost their lives or were fighting to keep them at that very moment. When the first building fell and the Pentagon was hit, I realized how catastrophic this event would be.

Like a child, all I could do was call my father 2,500 miles away. He picked up the phone mechanically without a word; somehow he knew he would hear my voice on the other end. I knew he would be awake and watching as I was.

"Daddy, are we being attacked?" I asked. I felt as though I had been time-warped back to childhood.

"I think so. Babe, you are going to be fine."

He said so with such a reassuring voice, I knew somehow it must be true. My dad would never steer me wrong.

Our hotel group was to be picked up at the front entrance of our hotel at 10:30 in the morning to go to the Convention Center for rehearsals and costume fittings. Four of us walked down in a daze.

"Did you see…?"

"Yeah."

We didn't have the strength to finish the conversation. We just held one another in disbelief on the way. We wondered to ourselves how all of this tragedy and turmoil would play out and how our nation would respond to the attacks. Upon arrival we were taken into the galley eating area where we waited for the other contestants to join us. We were the last group to arrive and many of the other women had been at the convention center during the attacks and only heard about them from the security guard personnel and by radio. They had yet to see the smoke staining the sky above the two fallen buildings.

Within moments of the time we were gathered together, I heard a cry I will never forget. It came from one of the Miss America staff members who received the phone call that changed her life (and mine) forever. We listened as she got the news that her cousin was the pilot of the jet that flew into the second tower. I could feel her pain as she sobbed. I joined her in weeping, not only for her agony, but for all the loved ones across the nation who were suffering for their lost ones. Miss Arizona, Kapri Rose, held me in her arms on the floor, and all I could say was, "I want to go home … I just want to go home."

We were quickly ushered into the rehearsal gym, Kapri holding me up as we walked and the events of the day unfolded. There, we were sequestered for the rest of the day. And it was there that our spines stiffened; we were not willing to permit terrorists to steal our hopes and dreams. like the rest of the nation, we would go on in remembrance of those who lost so much.

I've always carried a journal and I believe one of the entries made on September 11, 2001 expresses the confusion and emerging resolve of every Miss America competitor:

"I just can't figure out why I am suppose to go through this all by myself, here, just hours away from New York City, Washington D.C., and where the fourth plane went down in Pennsylvania. Here I am, right in the center of this, at the Miss America Pageant, some 2,500 miles away from my home, my family, and all of those I love. Why am I supposed to be here?

"This changes the whole dynamic of Miss America. It changes my whole outlook. I am no longer nervous about my interview. What's to be nervous about? It's not like it's going to kill me, or shake our nation, nor our lives; it's just a pageant. All of this puts everything into perspective for me. But I know that God created us all for *such a time as this.*"

All of those questions I posed to myself in my journal on September 12th have somehow been answered for me during my year as Miss Idaho. The roles and responsibilities of state title-holders have been dramatically and forever changed because of what we experienced at Miss America. Compassion for people and our nation, selflessness and pulling together as Americans — these are the most important lessons all of us at Miss America have learned. And, so has our country learned that we must never forget what we have seen, what we have heard, and how we felt.

Miss Illinois
2001

Kristin Marie
Castillo

Peace at Home

*T*here are certain events in our lives from which our memory will not let us escape. These events linger, as if locked into our minds by some mysterious force. For some, these memories may be the marriage of a family member or the birth of a child. But for all of us, there is one memory that we have in common — the tragedy that changed the world on September 11. For the rest of our lives, those events will remain lodged in our consciousness, never to be erased.

For me, it was the morning before our second rehearsal in Atlantic City. I was awakened by the sound of my pulsating alarm clock. I slipped out of bed, exhausted, just as I had done every morning before. After a breakfast of grapefruit and oatmeal, I rushed to prepare for the tiring day that awaited me. I hastily gathered my belongings and made my way to the small enclosure where the sink was situated. I stood in front of the mirror brushing my teeth, and I can clearly picture the expression on my traveling companion's face as she suddenly burst into my room.

"Kristin, turn on the TV right now," she said frantically.

Something was desperately wrong and I quickly turned on the television. At that moment, I saw the second plane crashing into the World Trade Center. No matter what station I turned to, I could not escape the grim image of destruction. In that instant, the magnitude of the events struck me, and I cried.

I watched as people ran hysterically from the collapsing monument; I watched as the police and firefighters bravely did everything they could to save as many lives as possible. I looked away, unable to view the disaster, after I saw the towers plummet to the ground, creating an ocean of rubble and death. The magnitude of the events and the human and symbolic cost were incomprehensible, but even at that time, I realized the repercussions would be unending and felt across the world.

For a brief moment, I looked outside my hotel window. The sky was cloudless, the day beautiful. The sunlight gleamed as it was reflected off the ocean, and I noticed sea gulls flying through the air seemingly unaffected by the mayhem that was happening merely miles away. There was a paradox in this. The sun shone as terror reigned, and it seemed as if nature was mocking us. I turned away from the window only to see once more, the stark contrast of destruction displayed on television.

I soon left my room to attend rehearsal as planned. Still shocked by what I'd seen, I entered the rehearsal area where all the contestants were gathered — grieving and traumatized. Uncertainty and terror ruled our minds, and so many questions remained unanswered. Concrete details about what was happening remained sketchy. Rehearsal was cancelled, and we spent the rest of the day huddled around a single radio. Somehow, as we gathered together, we felt an unexpected sense of comfort. We found strength in each other, and hope in the fact that the 51 of us were facing the unknown together.

My confused feelings at the time can best be expressed by an excerpt from my journal. On the evening of September 11, I wrote the following:

"Words do not convey the landslide of emotions tumbling chaotically through my mind. Destroyed by hate, the shattered remnants of New York's pride now rest in a sea of death. As the world unites, I ask myself, 'Where do I fit in? How can I help?' Horror, shock, bewilderment — how could this happen?"

Now, however, I look back on the beautiful day and the wheeling sea gulls, and it seems that rather than being a mockery of the disaster, it was a sign of hope for the people of the United States. Since the tragedy, much has changed for the better. Still, in the beginning things were difficult for us, as each of the contestants returned to her home state carrying with her a responsibility to do what she could to encourage the people she encountered.

I began my school speaking tour in October, less than one month after September 11. As I traveled across Illinois, from inner-city Chicago to the rural communities, I saw the diversity of my state's people. Yet no matter where I was, I noticed a common trait, a uniform display of strength, sense of unity, and commitment to our nation. In some cases it took a more violent and xenophobic turn, but true patriotism and Americanism were also more evident. People wanted to do whatever they could. More of them began to get involved in their communities, support charities, and demonstrate an overall feeling of goodwill toward fellow human beings. Also wanting to do my part, I took the opportunity to use the platform that the Miss Illinois Scholarship Program had given me to do what I could.

As Miss Illinois, I took notice of the fact that because of the renewed spirit of integrity among Americans, I found that my platform of Violence Prevention was more openly received. People who, before the attacks, would have brushed off the importance of violence prevention, now seemed to cling to any sign of peace.

Our government is pursuing this goal — peace — by waging a war to prevent terrorism and protect the American people. At the same time, however, there is another war being fought within the United States, in our own cities, communities and schools. The casualties of this war are the victims of homicide and suicide — the second and third leading causes of death for youths aged 15–24. While many of our military are fighting abroad, we must fight for peace at home. We cannot let our defenders risk their lives abroad for a peace at home that does not exist. We must do more to make peace in our homes, schools, and communities. After

September 11, this war on two fronts has become more visible and has served as motivation for involvement.

From my work as Miss Illinois, I have also witnessed people taking greater interest in matters reaching beyond the boundaries of this country. They have realized that never again can we withdraw into the bubble that we call "The United States of America." September 11 has wrenched us from peaceful oblivion and thrown us into the midst of world turmoil. This makes turning away from conflict no longer an option. Instead, as Americans, we have the responsibility to stand together as a symbol of hope and strength; as Americans, we have the responsibility to transform ourselves and our nation into the epitome of peace, compassion, and understanding; and as Americans, we must be the model of harmony that this world so desperately needs. Together, through the positive decisions that we make, we will counter the hate that is at the root of the September 11 tragedy.

Miss Indiana
2001

Allison Hatcher

The Power of Prayer

*T*he title of Miss Indiana isn't only about a beautiful crown. As Monica Hardin, Miss Kentucky said to me, "This isn't the only crown we will wear. One day it will be a heavenly one."

I have always believed in the power of prayer, but praying in public is often a touchy issue. This has not been the case since the terrorist attacks. People I spoke to were pleased when I bowed my head and prayed, and that became a ritual closing of my Miss Indiana appearances, and they showed their appreciation with warm smiles, nods, and heartfelt "Thank-Yous".

I come from a family that holds big annual reunions. To us family connections are the bonds that give each of us relevance and a strong sense of belonging. My mother, a minister, was born into a family of seven and from her I learned reverence for God and the passion to make His eternal light the lamp that guides me through the dark times and the good ones.

My dad, one child in a family of 13, is the parent from whom I inherited my love of music. He is the lead singer in a band and he encouraged me to make music the expression of my life. With that kind of an example, I learned to play the saxophone in concert, became a drum major in my school marching band and was a pianist for our church when I was 25.

Both Dad and Mom gave me the confidence in my courage to compete in beauty pageants leading to the title, Miss Indiana. Raising my self-esteem through achievements, working to win was the secret my folks gave to me. When you believe in yourself, almost anything is possible. because of the faith they had in me, I became versatile in music, teaching piano by the time I was 13, and I learned to be a long distance runner. I found the great satisfaction of celebrating the physical precision of my body when I flew like the wind rushing above the ground.

Another strong influence in my life has been my older brother who watched over me like a hawk when I was young. I remember an awful moment when my grandfather died. I thought about my mom losing her dad, and at the funeral had another terrible thought: what if I woke up, and my brother, my big protector, was dead? It was a terrible idea and it almost made me sick. He was the one who kept me safe from guys who wanted to hurt me. He was the one who wouldn't let me date a boy of whom he didn't approve. He was my guardian and he inspired me in his own way to be everything that I could be.

With these kinds of devoted cheerleaders in my family who rooted for me to win, how could I not become Miss Indiana? And as I competed later in Miss America, and after the event, I saw a reflection in hundreds of children I spoke to of how my own family role models were present in me. Just like me as I was growing up, children need people in whom they can trust and hold up as examples of the virtues and accomplishments the kids want to emulate. That's how we become bigger in ourselves, I have learned.

If I discovered anything at the Miss America Pageant, it was the truth of what I just wrote. My sisters in the class of 2001 recognized that they could be messengers of courage to their countrymen and women who were a little dazed by the terrorists' attack and needed to be reminded of who they were and what their country stood for. Service to others is the best gift to give and it is the one blessed by God. It was Robert Browning who put this in perspective when he wrote:

> *"All service ranks the same with God.*
> *with God whose puppets, best and worst, are we;*
> *there is no last or first."*

I am grateful for my year as Miss Indiana and I will continue to serve God by raising people up through my music which is a form of prayer. The nineteenth century poet, James Montgomery, expressed this idea so nicely when he wrote:

> *"Prayer is the soul's sincere desire,*
> *Uttered or unexpressed,*
> *The motion of a hidden fire*
> *That trembles in the breast.*
> *Prayer is the burden of a sigh,*
> *The falling of a tear;*
> *The upward glancing of an eye,*
> *When none but God is near."*

Miss Iowa
2001

Erin Smith

The Shadow of September 11

"Now pull!" I yelled, and three fourth graders back-to-back-to-back with linked elbows tried to walk forward in three different directions, tumbled over each other and landed in a tangled heap. The rest of the school assembly laughed and the threesome grinned sheepishly from the gym floor.

"If the three branches of our government each tried to go its own way without thinking about the other two, nobody gets anywhere," I explained to the crowd. "But when they work together and decide on one direction, they can really move."

The three students stood up and resumed their outward-facing triangle. I instructed them to move cooperatively toward the gym door and they easily scuttled across the floor, this time, prompting the entire audience of elementary students and teachers to break into applause.

"Let's have one more hand for Matt, Kelly, and Madison, who are representing our legislative, executive, and judicial branches," I called, renewing the applause as the kids found their way back to their seats.

The gymnasium was hot and the bleachers cramped, but every kid in that school was smiling. We were finishing a Miss Iowa assembly, and in less than half an hour the students had witnessed an interactive civics lesson that had them jumping out of their seats to volunteer for the role-playing skits, gasping in amazement at our citizenship fun facts, and most importantly, learning about the things that make our country a great nation.

The idea for Miss Iowa visits that coupled literacy with citizenship stemmed from the combination of circumstances following my return to Iowa after the Miss America competition. The events of September 11 made it obvious that how I would pursue my year of service in my home state had shifted. Educators were requesting programs that addressed issues like national unity and citizenship. I was looking for a way to link my established platform of children's literacy to my passion for patriotism, and my desire to inspire it in young students. Everyone was rooting for a way to make the project as positive as possible.

Fortunately, literacy lends itself readily to a wide range of topics. Merging books with citizenship was almost as easy as convincing schools to invite me to present the program to their students. My "Readers of Today, Leaders of Tomorrow" literacy initiative, in its infancy when I left for Atlantic City, blossomed into a comprehensive approach to interactive learning based on literacy fundamentals. Immediately after we developed a series of programs for different age levels. Soon, we had schools begging to be included. Armed with programs ranging from reading a book called *The Pledge of Allegiance* to kindergartners, to giving full-school assemblies on how our government works, I made hundreds of school visits across the state.

The visits were our way of putting a positive spin on the worst imaginable situation. We tried to make the presentations enjoyable as well as informative. One particularly popular element was the segment entitled "Ask Erin Anything," during which we challenged the kids to ask me questions about the United States government. As a political science major at Truman State University and a trivia enthusiast, I wasn't often stumped. In fact, after dazzling the crowd with my repertoire of useless U.S. trivia, children would sometimes ask me if being the Miss America Scholar meant that I was the smartest person in America. I usually said yes.

We rewarded inquisitive minds by allowing any student who came up with a question I couldn't answer, to come down out of the bleachers and add his name to a list. After my visit, I looked up the answers to those imponderables, and sent the kids a personal letter with the response.

Incidentally, the questions that elicited letters were things like, "How many presidents have had pet dogs?" and "What are the names of all of the Chief Justices of the Supreme Court we've ever had?"

Each school — like each day of a job like this — was different, but usually I left behind a room full of kids who were excited about reading and excited about America. I cannot begin to describe how fulfilling it is to have such a positive influence on so many audiences. Even more satisfying, perhaps, were the thank-you notes from children that recounted the things they had learned, or the letters from teachers that described how their kids still talked about the presentation months after I had been there.

One of the other big successes of the program was the manner in which we funded these activities. Our community-based corporate partners provided grant funding for all aspects of the program, eliminating the hardship many schools face trying to finance outside programs. In addition to direct donations of just under $11,000, we had the invaluable benefit of in-kind advertising donations in print and on television to help raise awareness of literacy issues and the "Readers of Today, Leaders of Tomorrow" initiative. Included were three sets of TV commercials with a combined eight-month run time, and quarter-page newspaper ads that ran for twenty-one weeks. The in-kind advertising and material donations were valued at nearly $88,000, bringing our fund raising total for the program to almost $100,000.

For skeptics of the merits of "pageant-based" programs, the volume of school visits and the fund raising efforts in particular proved to be strong evidence that gave communities in Iowa confidence in our ability to produce meaningful results.

The shadow of September 11 extended far beyond the harrowing weeks in Atlantic City, but the silver lining of such a horrific cloud was that it provided a powerful impetus to take a proactive approach to doing something good. Without September 11, would I still have been as enthusiastic about working with children? Probably. Would I still have channeled that enthusiasm towards promoting patriotism? Probably not. I would never dream of arguing that the benefits of renewed patriotism offset the tragedy of so many lives lost. I would, however, argue that the true strength of our nation likes in our resilience and our determination to make the best of the worst situation.

If the terrorist attacks shattered our way of life as we knew it, then our collective resolve made a mosaic of those shards. I strongly believe that God has a plan for everything, and it crushes my heart to think that such a tragedy could be part of His divine plan. I am convinced, though, that it is our duty to use that day for the betterment of ourselves, both as individuals and as a people.

"Before September 11," a student told me, "only basketball and baseball players were allowed to be heroes. Now we let policemen and firemen be heroes, too." Had it not been for the heroism of the men and women who worked to save the lives of strangers, we might have forgotten those attributes of a genuine hero.

"I like that so many people have the American flag in their window now. It's like everyone has the same decorations," said a third grader.

Had it not been for the renewed patriotism and national pride exhibited across the country in the following days and weeks and months, we might not have witnessed true national unity in our life times.

"You mean all those people died so that our lives could be the way they are?" asked a young boy, looking at pictures in a book about war memorials. "I had no idea our lives were worth that much!"

"Yes," I told him.

Had it not been for the thousands of Americans who unwittingly gave their lives, we might have never realized the value of our own.

Miss Kansas
2001

Kimberlee Grice

A Song of Pride and Honor

I have a confession to make. I've always hated singing the national anthem. From a singer's standpoint, it is one of the most difficult songs to sing. It reaches a full octave and I always have to start it at the lowest point in my range to be able to make the second half sound decent. On top of that, everyone in America has heard some of the greatest singers of our time perform it. There is no way that I could ever compete with the divas of the 20th century when it comes to this song. Plus, everyone knows the words and I always mixed them up. I never got nervous performing in front of a captive audience, but this was the exception. I cringed every time someone asked me to sing our national anthem.

Then I became Miss Kansas in June of 2001. My long road of singing in just about every little town along the wide open plains of the Midwest had just begun, and with it the many requests for the national anthem. I considered it torture.

But there were bigger things to worry about. Miss America Pageant was coming up, and the once-in-a-lifetime opportunity to compete for the title, and thousands of dollars in scholarship money. I was nervous about my wardrobe, my interview, my makeup, my weight, my talent, my pictures, my walk, my paperwork, and meeting the other women who were worrying over the same things. I had competed in the Miss Kansas Pageant for four years before I won.

Through my journey of becoming Miss Kansas, I had met the most amazing young women who became some of my closest friends. I was hoping the same would happen with my Miss America competitors.

People all around me assured me that I was going to be a strong competitor. I wanted to believe them, but I knew that there were fifty other women who were being told exactly the same thing. I had an inspiring platform in which I believed whole-heartedly. Just like most of my Miss America sisters, my platform chose me. My little brother had been killed in an auto-mobile accident in December 2000. At the tender age of eighteen, he was so full of life and hope. It only seemed appro-priate that he became a tissue donor. Once I found out about his life-saving gift, I made it my personal mission to educate and inform others about it. My platform of Organ and Tissue Donation Awareness was born.

When I arrived in Atlantic City, the dreams I had about Miss America were finally being realized. I had only known my new "sisters" for a few days, but I could tell that this was going to be one of the most amazing and life-changing events of my life. The repre-sentatives from the various states were as diverse as one could imagine. Each one was intriguing, insightful, and intelligent. Plus, they were all fun to be around. I was comfortable and enthusiastic about what the future held for us.

But those feelings quickly disappeared on that bright sunny day when it seemed like the sky was falling in on us. September 11 brought the devastating news that America was under attack and it wasn't soldiers fighting for their lives, but innocent people trapped in the rubble of the World Trade Center and the Pentagon. I remember seeing the images flash on my television screen in my upscale hotel room and knowing what it all meant. This meant war.

Losing a brother, I knew what it was like to grieve. I know what it's like to ask God all those questions, but never know the answers. I cried for the nation that day because we had lost so much.

In the same way, I knew what it was like to come back after a tragedy — to move on, and discover that you had become stronger. I prayed for that kind of experience for America. That we could fight, never forget, and become stronger in realizing what is really important.

The pageant continued after we decided that it should go on. Strangely, I no longer cared how I did. I was just thrilled to have the opportunity to be there. It was inspiring to see my competitors turn into lifelong friends. We had to rely on each other for strength, and we became our own family. When another name was announced as a finalist, I cheered and cried with each one. The competitive spirit was gone, and something else amazing took its place.

When I returned home after the Miss America Pageant, I was so very proud of my home state of Kansas. There was not one house without an American flag out front. There was even a huge billboard in big letters shouting "Kansas Loves NY". It was apparent that the entire nation felt the shock waves from NY and DC. No matter the distance, the nation grieved together just like the fifty-one state representatives did at the Miss America Pageant.

Everywhere I went to sing, the theme was patriotic. From local pageants to Christmas parades, the red, white and blue reigned supreme. I had to pull out the old standards like *God Bless America,* and *America the Beautiful.* Of course, everything started with the national anthem.

The first time I sang the *Star Spangled Banner* after September 11, was in my home town of Ulysses, Kansas. It was for a basketball game and the stands were packed with fans. As I stood in the middle of the giant court laced with orange and black and an image of a raging tiger glaring back at me, I felt the old nervousness of my phobia return. I knew these people would understand if I butchered this song — but I didn't want to.

The song meant something now. The words no longer described the bravery of history book soldiers, but of everyday people who were on their way to work one sunny September day. It spoke of the fire fighters and the police officers who lived and died to save their comrades. The bombs bursting in air were no longer in a painting of a fort hundreds of years ago, but of a plane crashing into the side of the building and all of it collapsing under its distorted weight and raging flames. The only flag that was still waving over the rubble of the fallen World Trade Center towers, was a piece of last week's newspaper. I sang our national anthem — I gave the best performance of my life.

No longer do I shrink from singing our national anthem anymore. In fact, I volunteer.

Oh, say can you see, by the dawn's early light,
What so proudly we hailed, at the twilight's last gleaming.
Whose broad stripes and bright stars, through the perilous
*   fight,*
O'er the ramparts we watched, were so gallantly
*   streaming.*
And the rocket's red glare, the bombs bursting in air,
Gave proof to the night that our flag was still there.
Oh, say does that star spangled banner yet wave.
O'er, the land of the free, and the home of brave.

Miss Kentucky 2001

Monica Hardin

We Stand as One

I'll never forget a visit I made before I became Miss Kentucky to the Eastern Kentucky Correctional Center. I was with a group called Creation's Prison Music Ministry and our purpose was to lift the spirits of inmates by singing gospel songs, country style music and contemporary Christian hymns.

It was a day in summer and was hot and it was my birthday, July 5th. I had been visiting prisons for about three years and spent every Christmas day cheering the convicts singing the old standards and favorites they requested.

On this day, I was walking in the exercise yard surrounded by dozens of men sentenced to hard time in this maximum security prison, accompanied by the prison chaplain. Something new was waiting for me.

Together we walked into the cheerless interior of the sturdy prison and descended to the lower level where convicts were imprisoned in "the hole" for breaking prison rules. Our heels echoed loudly on the hard polished cement floors and our voices, subdued by the gloom, the oppressive silence and the thick walls that closed us in, seemed smaller. I felt the solid weight of that prison pressing in on me, and knew for a moment the panic every convict must feel when he is locked inside an eight-by-eight solitary cell in the dark, with no light, no sound but his thoughts, and the small slot in his steel door which opened only for water and food to be passed through.

I sang *Amazing Grace* for those men with my words bouncing against the walls like desperate birds blindly seeking the light. And that was the moment, with tears running down my face, that I knew the answer to why I am here. What is my purpose in life? It was to serve. I knew I had brought hope to those for whom it meant a glimpse of sunshine, a song to cheer a desperate heart.

I've never forgotten that visit, for it gave me a sense of balance when two years later I became the third, and youngest, black American to be named Miss Kentucky.

I was born in South Louisville, Kentucky, learned I had a voice I could train, and worked on it through high school and then college at the University of Louisville where I majored in political science.

If my song for the men in solitary confinement two years earlier had been a moment of inspiration for me, it also was the leavening that made it possible for me to feel comfortable in the company of more fortunate and celebrated people. One was Secretary of State, Retired General of the army, Colin Powell who came to Louisville last November, following the disaster of September 11.

He was invited by the McConnell Center for Political Leadership of the University of Louisville. I was honored as a McConnell Scholar to sing *God Bless the USA*. Secretary Powell spoke of America and it was uplifting and reassuring. After his address, I was contacted by a man who identified himself as the song writer, Phillip Fletcher, and he told me he was so impressed by my voice and the passion for America that came through in my song, that I should have my own to sing.

And that's what happened. *No Place Like America* was the song he wrote for me to sing and the lyrics express my feelings for the country I love and represented at Miss America in Atlantic City.

With the permission of Phillip C. Fletcher and Rodney Noble, who wrote the music, here are the first three stanzas:

> *Out of many, we are one,*
> *a nation of people, called Americans.*
> *from different persuasions we've come to her shores,*
> *seeking a life of choice.*
> *Out of many, we stand ... as one,*
> *a nation of people, indivisible,*
> *we come from many distant shores,*
> *seeking a life that's full.*
> *e pluribus unum, my heart cries out,*
> *there's no place like America,*
> *there's no place like America.*
>
> *A nation of liberty,*
> *my home land, my country,*
> *her harbors, an open door, for so ... many.*
> *e pluribus unum, my heart cries out,*
> *there's no place like America,*
> *there's no place like America.*

Six months after September 11, I was on a plane headed for Washington D.C., playing out my role as Miss Kentucky in the company of the Kentucky delegation of Conversations with Youth to the National 4-H conference. As I thought back, I felt a remarkable sense of wonder that I had been so much a part of Miss America. More importantly, I had joined in the patriotic spirit of my sisters in the Miss America class of 2001 to spread the word that the assault against our country, far from making us fearful, or defensive about our ideals, has reinforced the iron in our creed of free speech, justice and equality for all.

I've come to know after talking and visiting with thousands of Americans that our strong institution of liberty is the lengthened shadow of our people and their devotion to our ideals. The reputation of one person is the lengthened shadow of his or her contribution to our country.

My job is to make the most effective contribution I can.

I plan to do that by working to develop a television talk show with international syndication that will feature people who will only speak about positive issues. A nineteenth-century woman whose grand words have been immortalized in print, Emily Dickinson, wrote a poem that expresses my passion to help other people find their way:

> *If I can stop one heart from breaking,*
> *I shall not live in vain;*
> *If I can ease one life the aching,*
> *Or cool one pain,*
> *Or help one fainting robin*
> *Unto his nest again,*
> *I shall not live in vain.*

Miss Louisiana 2001

Kati Guyton

Strength to Fly

*T*he story of how the butterfly changes from a caterpillar into a winged beauty has always fascinated me. As a young girl my mother often told me about this remarkable transformation. Although the caterpillar seems small and insignificant, there is an unbelievable plan for this living thing. It starts when she attaches herself to a leaf, spins a cocoon around herself, and while she is sheltered inside, a marvelous change takes place. She emerges as a different creature altogether.

Like the caterpillar, we, too, can make a miracle of ourselves. It comes from the strength we acquire by overcoming barriers and obstacles to our growth.

Because of a childhood growth disorder, I thought I would never become anyone of importance. Little did I realize that God would make a little miracle out of me if I chose to believe in myself. From the elation and the happiness created by winning Miss Louisiana 2001, to the shock and horror created by the loss of lives during the terrorist attacks on America on September 11, for me it has been an incredible opportunity. I have learned so much while traveling many miles throughout my state. I've come to understand that the obstacles we face can be overcome, and that the strength we gain from those experiences can make a difference when we use it to help the lives of others.

I do believe that God has a definite plan for each of our lives. I believe that He knew exactly what was going to happen in my life before I was born. But I had to grow and work on myself to fulfill His plan for me.

It took me four years to earn the title of Miss Louisiana. During those years, I planned for the day I would compete for the Miss America title. Little did I know that the Miss America Pageant would be dramatically different from any previous one. It wasn't certain that the event would happen. Finally, we voted to continue the pageant and the live television performance under extreme security conditions, and under a cloud of uncertainty regarding the availability of transportation at the time we would return home.

Together, we took the changes in our stride. For we had been transformed. We were less concerned with *me* and more focused on *we*. We had to handle our difficulties in a manner that would lift the Miss America Organization to a new high, and more importantly, we hoped to convince Americans that our job was to inspire people to transform their lives.

We are not butterflies, but in each of us there is the courage to transform, to overcome obstacles and to reassert our pledge of individual liberty in defiance of any kind of terrorism.

That is the real lesson in my mother's story of the caterpillar.

Miss Maine
2001

Meranda Rene
Hafford

The Power of True Spirit

*T*he night I was crowned Miss Maine, I could imagined the strength and powerful purpose of the message that I would be spreading throughout the state of Maine and beyond.

My goal of becoming Miss Maine was completely focused on earning the opportunity to serve as an activist for one year, on behalf of the D.A.R.E. (Drug Abuse Resistance Education) program — for which I had worked for seven years. Also, I wanted to benefit from the Miss Maine and Miss America scholarships programs and to use my voice to speak out on the choice of higher education and scholarship. I did so much with the D.A.R.E. program. The position of Miss Maine would open new doors and provide endless opportunities for me to work with students, schools and communities.

Arriving in Atlantic City as a Miss America contestant was absolutely amazing. I had to pinch myself to make certain that I was really among so many talented, beautiful, and goal-oriented young women competing for the Miss America title. I had watched the pageant for years, but never once believed that one day I would perform and walk on that stage. This was a true honor.

I researched topics for months in preparation for my personal interview, and had prepared myself mentally and spiritually for what the job of Miss America would be like if I won. I was healthy, in good physical shape and had the endurance to take on the duties of Miss America. Like every other state contestant, I was ready to become Miss America and be a national activist for my personal platform. I knew that this goal for which I had shaped myself had formed me into the person I was when I reached Atlantic City.

In the electric and solemn days after we learned about the shameful terrorist attacks in New York, Washington D.C. and a downed airliner in Pennsylvania, we gathered to discuss with officials of the Miss America Organization what the focus of Miss America should be, and how we could support the victims of disaster. Miss America would become a new symbol in our nation of solidarity and a refreshed pledge of respect for the values of our country.

I know that each of us participated with more zest in the revised program than we ever thought we could. We felt privileged to be competing during a time when our country needed to see examples of hope and encouragement from young people.

On September 22, as Katie Harman became our new Miss America. We knew that while she served as an activist for the breast cancer community, she would also carry the message of pride, hope for a brighter tomorrow, and reinvigorated allegiance from every American to make our country stronger and its citizens more aware of the privilege of democracy. What a remarkable job she has done.

When I returned to Maine people asked me, "Are you upset about not winning Miss America?" I smiled and said, "No. I am proud to be Miss Maine. God chose the perfect woman to be Miss America. It is my purpose to share her message with the people I speak to and my own about D.A.R.E."

Never once have I thought, "If only I had done that better, I might have won." No one in our Miss America 2001 class could have anticipated how greatly the role each of us would play when we returned home to a brighter, more intense purpose. That

September day, though tragic, helped me to better understand the meaning of "Miss Maine" and the message that I would share everywhere I went.

All the friendships I made while I was at Miss America have created a special sisterhood, one that embraces relationships and communication that will last for a lifetime. I am proud of all that my Miss America sisters have accomplished during their year of service. I was honored to carry their stories and messages with me while I spoke and reminisced about Atlantic City.

An excerpt from a note written by an extraordinary woman, Charlotte Gilman, before she died in 1935, summarizes for me, and I believe for all of my new sisters, the promise we embraced when we left Atlantic City for our homes:

"Human life consists of mutual service. No grief, pain, misfortune, or 'broken heart' is an excuse for cutting off one's life while any power of spirit remains."

Miss Maryland 2001

Kelly Glorioso

The Day the World Changed

*O*n the morning of Monday, September 10, 2001, I rushed around my hotel room in a flurry of activities. After an event-packed weekend in Philadelphia where I met my Miss America "Sisters" from across our country, I prepared for the train ride into Atlantic City, New Jersey, home of the Miss America pageant.

I was a young woman who had dreamed of participating in Miss America competition since a day in 1992 when, as a twelve year old girl, I traveled to Atlantic City to take in the Miss America spectacle. I stood on the runway after the conclusion of the telecast, and promised myself that I would work hard to realize my dream of representing my home state of Maryland one day.

Nine years and more than $30,000 in scholarship funds later, there I was on September 10, finally traveling to Atlantic City as Miss Maryland 2001 and a candidate for Miss America 2002. It was living up to everything I hoped it would be. I was thrilled to pull up to the train station to the song *There She Is,* which is as married to the event as the crown and the big bouquet of red roses.

When we got off the train, we were greeted by New Jersey's governor. A few relatives and friends had driven to Atlantic City to meet me and attend our opening press conference. The rest of the day was filled with photo shoots and settling into our hotel rooms. Everyone was excited and eager to begin rehearsal for the production numbers the next day.

I woke on Tuesday, September 11 to a beautiful clear sky and a room service breakfast tray to supply me with the fuel to meet what lay ahead. I settled in front of the television and was checking out the *Today Show* with my traveling companion, Belinda, when horror flashed across the screen. We saw a shot of one of the World Trade Center twin towers billowing clouds of smoke. Minutes later, I watched in frozen terror as a jet crashed right into the second tower.

Despite an overwhelming sense of unreality, horror and sadness, I still had to go to the convention hall that morning for group rehearsal. When I arrived and saw the other contestants — the expression on their faces mirrored my own. We turned to each other for comfort, and it was truly the next best thing to family. I know that the general public hears rumors about catty and vindictive pageant contestants sabotaging other candidates, being rude, and doing whatever it takes to win the crown. I only wish the naysayers could have seen our group of fifty-one crowding around the television that day, bonded like sisters.

Back in my hotel room that evening, I recorded the day's events in my journal. I had heard my grandfather, a World War II veteran, speak of the attack on Pearl Harbor and suddenly I understood the meaning of the words "A Day of Infamy." I knew then, as I know now, that living in fear and succumbing to the threats and actions of terrorists would eliminate life as we knew it.

I was ready, providing we demonstrated proper respect and patriotism, to continue preparing for the telecast scheduled a week and a half later. I went to sleep exhausted but ready to do my part and make our presence in Atlantic City as worthwhile as possible. Of course, the other young women had come to the same conclusion.

A little over a week later, on Saturday night, I believe we knew we had made the right decision, when our class of fifty-one young women stepped upon the stage at the beginning of the Miss America telecast. There was in all of us a great sense of celebrating America and all that is good about growing up in our wonderful country: freedom, education, service and success.

With the crowning of Katie Harman as our new Miss America, I knew that we had a fine ambassador who would do an incredible job of touring our country and giving her best effort to aid in the process of healing and rebuilding the spirit that is America.

As Miss Maryland, I have attempted to do my own part to aid in that effort. Among the many appearances I made each week, the most gratifying ones were those that honored our veterans, fire fighters, and those individuals who serve as every day heroes. Every time I sang the national anthem, I felt the power of our country's unity, and I will never forget the time when a crowd of five hundred people at a children's benefit joined in with such power and feeling, that I was breathless as we sang the last line.

At nearly every speaking engagement, I describe the strength and sisterhood I experienced at the Miss America pageant, which boosted my energy and determination to serve the people of my state and my country.

On September 11, 2001, I realized how much America, our citizens, and freedom truly mean to me. And I know that all my Miss America 2001 sisters feel the same way.

Miss
Massachusetts
2001

Abbie Lynne
Rabine

Blessings in Disguise

*P*eople are often curious to watch the response, and hear the perspective of the person announced first runner-up at Miss America, for she is the one who must come forward "if for any reason the winner cannot fulfill her responsibilities." On September 22, 2001, millions of viewers watched as I came first after Miss America 2002, Katie Harman. I am proud to say that what others may have viewed as my misfortune to place second, I perceived as a character defining moment and an opportunity to strengthen my resiliency. This conviction was heightened by the historic disaster on September 11, 2001 that challenged a nation to convert a tragedy to triumph and to demonstrate our perseverance.

Unaware of the transformation we were about to experience, fifty-one young ladies fell fast asleep the night before dreaming of winning the coveted rhinestone crown. I remember applying the finishing touches of ravishing red lipstick the next morning when I was interrupted by my traveling companion, Buffy, frantically screaming, "a plane has just crashed into the World Trade Center!"

Shocked and stunned, we glued ourselves to the television, and listened to Katie Couric try to explain the unbelievable. Unsure of what to do, we joined Miss New York, Andrea Plummer; Miss Delaware, Erin Copper; and Miss Texas, Stacey James, in the lobby of our hotel. We waited to be driven to the convention hall for morning rehearsals. Eventually, pageant officials gathered us into the convention ballroom. Due to the state of confusion, I honestly cannot recollect whether we watched television like other Americans, returned to our hotel rooms waiting for further direction, or discussed the future of the pageant. I can only remember my fragmented prayer, "Lord, we can't — you can. Please do!"

Desperate to phone my family, I hoped for word of my brother, Jeremy Wayne Rabine, E-6 Staff Sergeant in the United States Marine Corp. After numerous attempts, I was connected to him. I asked him what he knew about the course of military action, and his opinion of whether or not we should continue with the Miss America pageant.

As long as I live I will remember my brother's response. "Abbie Lynne, it is my belief that we are placed where we are during such a moment to encourage and inspire a nation of leaders."

When he said those words, I knew his job was to bear arms, and protect America and mine was to unite with my Miss America sisters and do our part to motivate our country to respond to the awful challenge like champions. I knew then also that the lesson I learned from an earlier personal challenge had great meaning for me now. At age ten, I was diagnosed with a language-based learning disability. My dreams and desires to be Miss America, a singer, and an educator seemed impossible because I stuttered and had to learn to control it. For twelve years I endured ridicule and embarrassment while laboring through speech pathology sessions. Persistence was its own reward and manifested when I was crowned Miss Massachusetts 2001, announced first runner-up to Miss America 2002.

The Miss America Pageant experience forever fortified my belief to serve others before self, to have hope in mankind and the faith to surmount our challenges.

Miss Michigan 2001

Stacy Lynn Essebaggers

Life Is Unpredictable

*E*xcitement and anticipation were at an all-time high as fifty-one strong, talented, intelligent, passionate, community-minded women embarked on an adventure of a lifetime when we stepped down from the train in Atlantic City. Each footstep we took became a step closer to living a dream. A marching band welcomed us and the familiar music, once again sparked a vision in each of our minds that one of us would become the new Miss America 2001.

"Am I actually here?"

September 11, 2001: A group of us arrived at Convention Hall at 8:30 in the morning for our first day of rehearsal. I remember walking by the Miss America stage, and I thought once again of how blessed I was to be here. A group of us had fittings that morning and upon returning to our dressing room, we heard the terrifying news of the terrorist attacks in New York and at the Pentagon. As we sunk into our chairs, disillusioned, a woman police officer explained the details. At first, I have to admit I was a little desensitized. In the past we've seen disasters take place — they are alarming, but how closely do they actually affect us?

As I sat there, trying to take everything in and understand how real everything was, I looked over at Marshawn Evans, Miss Washington D.C., glanced over at Andrea Plummer, Miss New York ... reality very quickly set in. As I looked at them, I felt the pain of not knowing: the fear and possibility of this event taking place in my state. The dressing room was so silent that you could hear a pin drop, and the color had drained from each one of our faces as we listened intently to the radio. We held each other's hands and prayed; our bond of sisterhood was formed at that very moment.

A day later, after the attack on the World Trade Towers in New York, I think we all realized that the job of Miss America and that of all the state representatives would change dramatically. Not only would each be a spokesperson for her cause, but she would be an ambassador of hope and strength representing a country in need of that very ideal.

Then came Monday, September 17th. I thought the worst was over. It was the night before the first preliminary competition and the one before my interview. I decided to go to the Tiara ballroom (of all places) to practice my clogging routine. I did my dance three times, but decided to do it once more to get a workout. On the fourth time, as I went into a turn, my ankle turned out. I heard a loud pop, then I crashed to the floor.

I sat there for a moment thinking, "Did this just happen?" I jumped to my feet and started walking briskly around the room. I was in disbelief and was not going to let this happen. The pain was too much to bear and I fell again. That night I was taken to the Atlantic City Trauma Center. The emergency doctor took one look at my x-rays and told me, "I'm sorry, but your ankle is broken."

I remember being driven back from the hospital that night feeling disheartened and wondering what I was going to do. It wasn't until about 2:30 in the morning that I realized something which would change my life. As I sat in my bed, with my temporary cast propped up on a pillow, water leaking all over from my ice bags, surrounded by darkness, I couldn't help but think of all I had seen on television the week before. I could picture in my mind all the people running through the streets, helplessly trying to find their family members and friends lost in the attack on the towers, and the children who would spend Christmas without their moms or dads.

I thought to myself, "Stacy, what you are going through is temporary. What you are facing is a temporary setback, but what those people in New York and Washington D.C. are facing, that's permanent."

At that very moment, I made a choice to go on. I also remembered something a good friend told me. "The body achieves what the mind believes." The next day I had my interview and afterwards went to see a specialist. I truly believe a miracle happened because he told me that I had popped a ligament and had a two-degree sprain. He advised me not to dance. I had to sign waivers relieving the Miss America Organization of any responsibility if I were injured while performing.

Wednesday night I danced, I performed and when I finished, I came back to a room of fifty of the most amazing supportive sisters cheering and smiling. I'll never forget that moment. I've thanked them many times in my mind for helping me accomplish something I never thought I'd be able to do.

The adversity we faced, as well as my own personal trial, made me think of what my mother went through fourteen years earlier. She had been diagnosed with breast cancer in 1988, underwent a full mastectomy, and has had awesome health ever since. She was faced with a choice every day while fighting breast cancer: either to let it consume her and give up or she could fight. She chose to stand up courageously and fight because she realized that she had a lot worth living for. Mom, you are an amazing woman!

Things surely happen for a reason, I know that now. God's plan for me was to come home to Michigan with a story. A story and message of hope, strength and empathy for all those who face adversity. Lastly, my experience at Miss America showed me that life is unpredictable: whether it happens as an attack on our country, whether a woman suddenly injures her foot before the

Miss America pageant, or someone has been diagnosed with breast cancer. We all face events that change our lives. That is why it is so important that we cherish every moment, and value highly the time we spend with our family and friends. Life is so very precious.

Miss Minnesota
2001

Kari Knuttila

The Crowning Points

*W*earing the crown of Miss Minnesota was a dream come true for me and perhaps the greatest honor of my life. To have the privilege and the responsibility of representing my home state at the Miss America Pageant was both tremendously thrilling and sincerely humbling. It did not take me long to understand that my reign as Miss Minnesota would have a great impact on my life, but it was not until September 11, that I realized how profound an experience it would be. For me and the rest of the Miss America contestants, life would take on a whole new meaning. There was one clear truth that struck me through this experience; God is in control. No one had any control over the terrible tragedy that took place on that day. I had no control over the outcome of the pageant. I had no control over whether or not my family would be able to make the trip to Atlantic City to cheer me on. In all of these situations, I could only extend my hand and allow God to lead me through.

At the Miss America Pageant I was particularly reminded of what was truly important in life by my family and friends who braved the airlines and flew to Atlantic City to support me. A total of 74 people from seven different states made the trip to be a part of this experience with me. Having that kind of unconditional love and support made me grateful beyond words. Each time before I stepped onto the stage, I was able to look directly at my cheering section with their "Minnesota Loves Kari" sign and feel my spirits lift.

Starting each day with prayer helped keep everything in perspective for all of us who were at Atlantic City. Take away the crown and the sparkling dresses and what people think of as a stereotypical "beauty queen," and you have the Miss America class of 2001. A dedicated, motivated group of women who are ready to take on the world and make a difference and we each had a chance to show that this year.

My platform "Music Makes a Difference," is not just an issue I talk about, it is my passion in life. I shared that passion when I returned to my hometown of Detroit Lakes to raise money for the music and arts programs at my alma mater. I performed and shared my love of music at many schools; at numerous communities speaking on the benefits and the importance of having music and arts education as a part of every school's curriculum. Through all of these appearances, not only was I able to increase awareness and appreciation for the arts, but I also was able to break through some of the stereotypes that go along with the stigma of pageants. Everywhere I went there were always a few skeptics in the crowd, but once I told my story about why Miss America is so vital and why the 51 of us decided to be involved in its scholarship program, many people were pleasantly surprised.

As a future teacher, I particularly enjoy speaking at schools. Many students and young people look up to me and I love it when they realize that I am not perfect and am just a normal person who is doing her best to do extraordinary things. My Miss America experience challenged me personally in so many ways! I have done things I never thought possible, such as getting up in front of 800 high school students and explaining not only the inspirational value of music, but also my faith in God. My experiences at Miss America and my year as Miss Minnesota have forever changed my life.

Every time I make an appearance as Miss Minnesota, I talk about my crown and why it is a symbol and reminder to me of what is important in my life. Each point on the crown has a special meaning to me. The first one is for my job as Miss Minnesota, and what I must accomplish during my reign. The second point is for all the people who helped me become Miss Minnesota because I could *not* have done it on my own. The third point on my crown is for each and every person whom I have had the opportunity to meet this past year. The crown and title have given me the opportunity to travel around the entire state and meet thousands of people and it is because of this third point that I am able to bring each person with me on my journey. The last point on my crown is the most important one and that is my faith. This point reminds me to not only "talk the talk," but "walk the walk." It reminds me that I am a role model and that people are watching how I act and what I say. I want to live the kind of life that I would want others to exemplify as well.

There are so many lessons in life I have been able to take away from my year as Miss Minnesota. I have learned lifelong skills that will help me be a better teacher, woman, citizen, and overall better person. I have learned about time management and what it really means to be busy! I have learned about the importance of independence as well as the need to lean on others. On top of all of this, I have gained scholarship funds to further my education so I can be a well rounded, effective music teacher.

This year has been part of a new lifelong commitment to service. I have been blessed beyond measure by these many experiences and lessons I have learned. A warm "Thank-You" to my Miss America sisters and other supporters for being a part of this journey.

Miss Mississippi 2001

Becky Pruett

Keeping the Spirit Alive

I will never forget the moment I saw the second plane hit. That is when I knew that my way of life would never be the same. It struck me as ironic that I was in Atlantic City competing for the title of Miss America when tragedy fell upon our great nation. How could I compete for a title when I wasn't even sure I grasped the true significance of its meaning? What did America mean to me?

I remembered stories from my grandfather who served in World War II. He spoke of patriotism and a sense of pride in one's nation. The heroes he talked about did not fit a mold, they could not be bought in a toy store, and they were not found on the big screen. The heroes in his stories were everyday men and women who gave selflessly without reward or fame. How I enjoyed my grandfather's stories.

However, on September 11, those stories took on a new meaning in my life; they became reality. I saw firsthand what it meant to love thy neighbor, to give the shirt off your back, and to pray for all of mankind. My experience during those troubling days was unique, if not blessed, because when I cried out from pain, confusion, and uncertainty, I had fifty of my Miss America sisters there to hear me. When I found out that my mother, a medical attaché officer at the American Embassy in Guinea, West Africa, would not be able to attend Miss America because her Embassy had been closed down due to potential threats from terrorists, some of the other contestants offered their own mothers as stand-ins for mine. Our bond was special and during that week, we began to heal as one nation under God.

Never will I forget my experience at Miss America. When I returned home to Mississippi, I realized the effects of that day were far-reaching. Throughout my year of travel as Miss Mississippi, I was able to use my crown as a vehicle for a powerful message of hope within my state. Every city, church and school I came to had one common theme; Mississippi and its people will not be broken.

I know this to be true because before and during my year as Miss Mississippi, I have been able to witness first hand how effective inspired people can be to influence young persons. It has been my privilege to work with Mississippi's Attorney General Mike Moore in his war against tobacco since I served as a youth advisor in the state's vigorous program of Tobacco Awareness for Minors.

It was Mike who was the first to win a four billion dollar legal settlement for Mississippi from the tobacco interests. It funded our statewide program to focus on convincing kids to abstain from cigarettes. And it certainly has been effective. We have been responsible for bringing about a twenty percent decrease in teenage smoking, a record that makes my favorite state a stand-out in the war against tobacco. I will never forget Mike's compliment when he said of me: "Becky championed the cause when it wasn't cool to do it."

I am grateful for the lessons I have learned from my Miss America experience during September 11. I believe that all of us have been given an extraordinary opportunity to prove that the spirit of America is alive and stronger than ever as we all walk together, hand-in-hand into each brand new day!

I know I am right about the spirit being alive and well because it has really never flagged. For proof of this, one has only to look back at the Americans who lighted the flame of liberty for all of us more than two hundred years ago. To me that spirit was immortalized by Henry Wadsworth Longfellow in his poem *Paul Revere's Ride,* with which many school children are still familiar. I've quoted excepts from that remarkable poem here.

Remember how it started —

You will recall how Paul was signaled by lantern from the church bell steeple and thundered through a dozen villages raising the alarm, until —

> *It was two by the village clock,*
> *When he came to the bridge in Concord town.*
> *He heard the bleating of the flock,*
> *And the twitter of birds among the trees,*
> *And felt the breath of the morning breeze*
> *Blowing over the meadows brown.*
> *And one was safe and asleep in his bed*
> *Who at the bridge would be first to fall,*
> *Who that day would be lying dead,*
> *Pierced by a British musket-ball.*
>
> *You know the rest. In the books you have read,*
> *How the British Regulars fired and fled —*
> *How the farmers gave them ball for ball,*
> *From behind each fence and farmyard wall,*
> *Chasing the redcoats down the lane,*
> *Then crossing the fields to emerge again*
> *Under the trees at the turn of the road,*
> *And only pausing to fire and load.*
> *So through the night rode Paul Revere;*
> *And so through the night went his cry of alarm*
> *To every Middlesex village and farm —*
> *A cry of defiance, and not of fear,*
> *A voice in the darkness, a knock at the door,*
> *And a word that shall echo forevermore!*
> *For, borne on the night-wind of the Past,*
> *Through all our history, to the last,*

In the hour of darkness and peril and need,
The people will waken and listen to hear
The hurrying hoof beats of that steed,
And the midnight message of Paul Revere.

Miss Missouri 2001

Jennifer Ann Hover

Full Time Job

*H*ow can I ever forget the thick pall of smoke that darkened the sky above the stricken World Trade Center Towers in New York. I could see it from my hotel window in Atlantic City after we learned of the attack on America. Also, I will never forget the next day when all of us met to decide the fate of the Miss America Pageant the words of Miss Oregon, Katie Harman. She said, "We have to realize that if we stay and continue, one of us is not going home in the end."

Several days later, she walked the runway as our new Miss America, and she was not going home. She was going to represent our great country in her travels. No less important, the rest of us would go home to be many things — patriots, leaders and role models.

In my state of Missouri, being the designated "Miss" is a full time job. It requires lots of travel by car to carry a new message of courage to people everywhere. I wondered what that would be like after the events which had transpired. We were going to war. Some of our countrymen and women (including two dear friends of mine) would go overseas while I would go out to encourage Missourians.

My first big challenge was speaking publicly about September 11. It was difficult not to become emotional. I was expected to be a rock and inspire, when all I wanted to do was cry and remember how horrible it was that day. I finally realized that it was okay to cry.

Whenever I made an appearance as Miss Missouri, I was usually allowed to speak for a few minutes and my speeches always had a similar theme. *Life is precious. Don't take even the little things for granted.* These words had always been a cliche until we were faced with a national tragedy.

I think now more than ever, people realize how wonderful it is to be alive and how amazing it is to be an American. I will never forget the young women at the Miss America Pageant. When we decided not to go home and carry on with the event, we became each other's family.

I will always be indebted to Becky Pruett, Miss Mississippi, for making me laugh until I hurt and for her incredible support and loving friendship to this very day. Marta Stryzweski, Miss New Mexico, showed great class and offered her friendship to me. Carolyn Dragoo, my second week traveling companion, boarded a plane just days after September 11, to be with me in Atlantic City. Mary Bybee, with whom I will always share a unique bond and relationship, is unforgettable. All of us, and my family and friends.

September 11, was an important event in our country's history, one of immense magnitude. It gave me a new sense of responsibility as an American. I was conscious of the fact that I have to set an example for every young person in my state. I decided to set goals for myself and I met every one of them.

Among the many speeches I gave, I am most proud of the one at a national conference for Youth Development which focused on the importance of self-esteem and positive peer pressure education in our schools. I also worked with Governor Holden on developing the first ever Missouri Youth Cabinet. I met and spoke to thousands of people, and received a special proclamation from my home town of Springfield, recognizing me for my accomplishments. All of this has been a great honor to me and my family. But my greatest accomplishment has been to touch the lives of so many people. Many boys and girls have written to tell me that I am their role model. I have met many of them. One little girl came to see me crown the new Miss Missouri. I took her downstairs to the dressing room to introduce her to all of our 2002 Miss Missouri contestants.

"Ladies, this is Megan," I said with great pride. "She is here tonight because we have become good friends during my year as Miss Missouri. She wants to be Miss America some day, and she is the reason you should want to become Miss Missouri tonight."

Megan is one of the reasons why I am most proud that we did not go home after September 11. If I had given up, I would have let her down. Instead, I can proudly say that I have been a good leader by making confident, healthy and, at times, brave choices for my year as Miss Missouri. Miss America may be the pep rally for the other fifty "Misses", but for me it was much more. It provided me with a heightened sense of patriotism and a stronger courageous spirit. It also helped me realize that I am not alone, that my new faith and pride is shared by a country of Americans.

Miss Montana 2001

Kara Svennungsen

Shall We Dance?

*W*here has the time gone? I lie awake tonight knowing that tomorrow I pass on this title of Miss Montana. I think back on a scrapbook of memories, and a year that changed me forever.

May of 2001 found me saying farewell to Gonzaga University and Spokane Washington. With a Public Relations/Broadcasting degree in tow, it was time for me to face the real world and find a real job. But after an emotionally draining final semester, I retreated to my home town of Shelby, to clear my mind and weigh my options under the big sky of Montana.

Shelby is tucked beneath the Canadian border in the western part of the Big Sky's high-line. Your typical small-town USA, it's a big family of about two thousand people. There are no stoplights, and everyone knows your name. Being embraced once again by the familiar warmth and friendliness of this small town, something stirred in me. At age twenty-three, I realized how blessed I was to have been raised in such surroundings. Becoming Miss Montana really wasn't one of the options I had been considering seriously, but the opportunity to serve my state was irresistible. In just a matter of weeks, I was crowned and I began my work as Miss Montana.

Attending the Miss America competition was my first big responsibility. A whirlwind of shopping, altering clothes, training and singing filled the next two months. Shelby and the surrounding area threw the classiest send-off barbecue in the county for me. When my supporters learned that the organization was a bit strapped for cash, they raised $9,000 in just three weeks. My heart was as full as my suitcases, and I was off to Atlantic City.

My breath caught in my chest as I entered the lobby of The Ritz Carlton Hotel and took in the fifty women who were to be my family for the next weeks. It seemed like a fairy tale with fifty-one lovely princesses, one of whom would be chosen queen. But reality quickly set in. The events of September 11 created a sobering change for us; I felt like a scared child. Our days were rooted in prayer and forged with the strength of our support for one another.

Representing our states took on new meaning. I could not wait to get back home.

Once I landed, I hit the highways and became a self-proclaimed "queen of the road." Using two cars, driving almost 50,000 miles, I gave 378 thirty-minute presentations to 50,300 students in 301 schools in 155 towns across Montana. I still can't believe it. Every day was a new adventure. I slept in the homes of generous, hospitable people, awoke under every inch of our Big Sky, and hastened to "work" each day in a country of breathtaking landscapes. Once, while driving through Paradise, Montana, at sunset, I glanced at my speedometer with surprise. Captivated by the beauty all around me, I was loafing along at 15 miles per hour. I am proud to report zero speeding tickets (two warnings) and no run-in with a deer — just one bird.

It was my purpose to make students realize how much their lives mattered. I urged them to share their gifts and give Montana a lift. "Life is not a dress rehearsal," I quoted. "You get only one chance. Will you sit it out or will you DANCE?"

My message was: I Hope You'll D.A.N.C.E. I explained that each letter stood for an action that each one should take to heart:

D - Decide to use your life — set your goals and go for
     it!
A - Act wisely by making healthy choices.
N - Never give up. When the going gets tough,
     Montanans get tougher.
C - Care for others. Never pretend you're too cool to
     care about your family, your friends and others.
E - Educate yourself and enjoy every day.

I reminded myself and my audiences that "Yesterday is history, tomorrow is a mystery, but today is a gift. And that is why we call it the present." I concluded my presentation with Lee Ann Womack's song *I Hope You Dance*.

My rewards came in the responses from the children: "Miss Montana, how much can you trade your crown for on ebay?"

Then there was the honest kindergartner who held up my photo and asked, "Were you a little younger in this picture?" I sure felt like it at that moment.

In Helena, Montana's capital city, I overheard a boy ask his teacher where Miss Montana was, as I stood center stage. I thought I must have had a bad hair day. But when his teacher pointed me out to him, he exclaimed, "That's Governor Judy Martz!"

Assurance that the students really heard my message came in hundreds of priceless letters they sent. They would recite the meaning of D.A.N.C.E., alert me to their accomplishments, and ask comical questions. A fifth-grader in Choteau wrote:

"Dear Miss Montana,
*   I am using my manners and working hard wrestling. I*
enjoy long walks on the beach at sunset, and you have
pretty blonde hair … I'm free Sunday — are you?"

One letter will touch me forever. In October, nine-year-old Morgan Wyrick, wrote me the dearest four-page note in pretty gel pen ink. At the end, her mother had attached a note saying that Morgan was being flown to Denver for a bone marrow transplant.

I e-mailed, prayed and was inspired daily by this angel's strength as I went on with my job. When I opened the newspaper on June 13th, and saw Morgan's obituary, my heart ached. I am forever reminded that every single moment and every person is so important. Life is short, and we have no business taking one minute for granted.

As the curtain closes, I park my car, turn off my microphone, and thank God for the opportunity of a lifetime. I have learned that knowledge of our mortality is a wonderful gift. Stock market low or cholesterol high, we have a wealth of riches in the American people and the land around us. And from New York City to Podunk, Montana, we need each other. In using our time and talents to serve our neighbors, we all dance. We make each day an American masterpiece.

Miss Nebraska
2001

Christina
Foehlinger

The Heartland

*T*o you who are reading this book, I would like to share an e-mail I sent to my family and friends on Tuesday, September 11. I think it best explains my feeling about the terror and destruction in New York and Washington, D.C.:

"Prayers, smeared make-up, silence, police escorts, empty streets, news reports, and fifty-one young women bound together by one common feeling of sorrow. Today is a day that will go down in the history books and change our life as we know it, as well as our future. I am lucky that no one close to me has been harmed, but my heart and prayers are with the individuals and their families who have been not so lucky.

"Am I frightened? Yes. Am I upset? Absolutely. Will I lose my faith? Never. There is a reason to understand why things like this happen, but I know that one thing is for sure. There is a reason for what happened today, just as there is a reason why I am here in Atlantic City at this time.

"What is my role? I am uncertain, but as Miss Nebraska, I will do my best to represent our state well out here, and express my sympathy for those who have been directly affected by this despicable terrorist attack on our country and our people.

"In all honesty, my focus has shifted from the pageant to more important events. I know that if you are in Nebraska right now, it may be hard to understand the magnitude of this disaster, but the empty streets and casinos of Atlantic city reflect the shock and sorrow and the mood of the people here on the East Coast. It is quite frightening.

"In closing, I want everyone who receives this e-mail to know that I love them, and that I hope they have not lost anyone close to them. Please do not worry about me here in Atlantic City. I feel very safe because of the amazing security personnel around us. To those of you traveling to Atlantic city soon; please be careful. My thoughts and prayers are with you all."

With the pageant over and with the memories of this event tucked away in my heart, I returned home to the heartland where I felt far safer than I did on the East Coast. I knew my role as Miss Nebraska had changed. My platform issue of Eating Disorder Awareness and Prevention became more effective because I used every appearance to promote patriotism, and express great pride for our country.

And, I wanted to do more. I decided that as Miss Nebraska I could use my title and influence to help in relief efforts for 9/11 victims. By using my talent and my love of performing, I could help earn money for the aid effort. So, I participated in many talent and variety shows staged for the 9/11 heroes and victims and their families.

Did my life change? Yes, in many ways. The Pledge of Allegiance holds new meaning for me now. *The Star Spangled Banner* continues to bring tears to my eyes. Fire fighters have become bigger-than-life heroes. I don't take as much for granted and I thank God everyday that my family was saved from harm. I can only hope as our nation struggles to deal with its loss, it will heal the wounds and become stronger than ever.

I am a Nebraskan. I live in a state somewhat removed from the centers of great activity, but when terror struck New York and

Washington D.C., we felt it just as deeply as those who were at ground zero. But to most accurately describe the feelings and emotions we dealt with in my part of the world, I have included a poem I wrote about how the terror of September 11 hit home in the heartland:

Heartbreak in the Heartland

No, we could not see the smoke shut out the sun,
But those in the Heartland felt the pain.
No, we could not watch the buildings fall,
We knew the world would not be the same.
A son, a daughter did not come home,
A farmer wipes his sweaty brow and bows his head
to pray.
We wept as we watched in horror,
How dare they try and take our freedom away.
Nebraska, Iowa, Kansas, Dakotas,
Tonight we sing by candlelight.
We cry for those who lost their lives,
God Bless our soldiers who must now fight.
We were not there, we did not see,
But remember we will.
On September 11th we were put to test,
Our patriotism they will not kill.

Miss Nevada
2001

Ashley Huff

Life's Lessons

*I*t seems like yesterday that I was standing on stage anxiously awaiting the announcement of the new Miss Nevada 2001. My heart was pounding so hard I could hear it beating. Tonight, I will crown the new Miss Nevada 2002. Standing backstage, I can see my reflection in a tall mirror. My crown is shimmering and sparkling in the bright lights of the stage, and I can't help but reflect upon the journey that brought me to this moment. I still feel as though my fairy tale Cinderella dream came true (and it went so fast). Standing here, I am proud of myself and of my family for all we have accomplished. I can clearly see some of life's important lessons in this moment, as they flash before my eyes.

I grew up in the South — a shy little girl — the youngest of seven children. We were each unique with different personalities, talents and interests. Our parents always encouraged us to develop the talents that God gave us, and to broaden our horizons and experiences. I was quite young when my mother realized my love of dance and the stage. She saw that performing was perhaps my opportunity to overcome my shyness. However, limited finances sometimes made it difficult for me to pursue the dance classes. But, somehow, my parents always made it happen by trading their talents or work for our lessons.

As a result, I learned that you never focus on the barriers, but on how to overcome them and make your goals happen. I have also learned at a young age that anything worthwhile usually comes with some adversity. I have become a young woman with goals, determination, and perseverance, and have learned to improvise and make the best of what I have been given.

I continued my involvement in the performing arts and earned a true respect and appreciation for cultural dance. This passion led me to audition for and being involved with the 1996 Olympic Opening Ceremonies. This experience was truly a defining moment for me, and helped me set my future goals. With the exposure to the press and the activities surrounding the athletes, it became clear to me that I wanted a career in television broadcasting. I loved being a part of the events that brought people from all over the world together. I was enthralled to see language barriers broken by dance and music. While this was one of the most thrilling events of my life, it was overshadowed by the Olympic park bombing and the crash of the TWA jetliner suspected to have been the result of a terrorist act.

The night of our final performance we entered the Olympic stadium with the greatest caution and heightened security, instead of the joy and exhilaration we should have brought to the opening ceremonies. Little did I realize the strong role that this experience would play in preparing me for the next, and, even more important event of my life — the Miss America Pageant. Both events reaffirmed for me that all worthwhile causes are usually preceded by adversity.

My experience in Atlanta gave me the courage, determination, and coping skills which I would need on September 11. It was on the first day of rehearsals, after I arrived in Atlantic City, that the attacks on our country occurred. The world had changed.

Attending the Miss America Pageant separated us from our family and friends. Thankfully, we had each other for support and comfort. Many of the pageant events were canceled and security was heightened. My recent challenge to get all my seventeen pieces of luggage to Miss America, tipping sky caps, and preparing for all the stages of competition suddenly seemed petty. The following days united all the contestants in a special bonding, and I made many lasting friendships in those troubled and painful times.

As I reflected about the road that led me to this pageant, I came to understand that each challenge met was a step forward. Moving to Las Vegas to attend the University of Nevada motivated me to promote my platform of sexual abstinence for teens. I spoke to a lot of school kids about that important subject, promoted the True Love Waits and STAR programs and encouraged the students to make positive life choices. My hard work paid off, and I was named Miss Nevada 2001.

Despite the controversial nature of my platform, the talks were well received, and I have always left my audience with the message: "Abstinence is not the most popular choice, but it is the best choice. It will give you the freedom and control to direct your life and the opportunity to make choices. The choices that you make today, will affect you for the rest of your life."

I was excited when I was nominated by Governor Kenny Guinn to be a spokesperson for the Nevada State Abstinence Works Program. I was also nominated for the Miss America Quality of Life award. Seven out of fifty-one girls were nominated. I was thrilled to know that this powerful and important message was recognized on a national level, and I would not change my platform, as I was advised, because of its controversial nature. Nor because it would not generate money for the Miss American scholarship program. I was told that a blonde, blue-eyed, Polynesian dancer from Las Vegas, the City of Lights, and from a state with legalized prostitution, did not make an appealing headline. Not to mention, that I worked for Victoria's Secret as a cosmetic consultant. Even with the pressure of jeopardizing my chances at the Miss America pageant, I knew that I had to stick with my choice; I could not give in to something that was not true to me.

I will admit, I was crushed and hurt when later my name was not called as a finalist. Watching my preliminaries on video, I was proud of my performances and of my convictions.

In the end, I am thankful to have had all of the special moments and wonderful experiences. I now know that my strength of character will not falter when tested. And I will never forget the young girl at the reception at Miss America Pageant who asked me: "How can you keep smiling when you lost?"

I have thought about the answer to that question many times, and I believe it would be: "Winning is exhilarating and uplifting, but it is the tradition of trying that matters which builds character and personal consequence."

Miss New Hampshire 2001

Katherine Lise Pike

Redefining Goals

*L*ast Friday, October 12, as Miss New Hampshire, I visited a middle school in Hampton, New Hampshire, where I spoke to 300 children from grade three to five about things that I believe are core to a child's development such as academics, extra-curricular activities and goal setting.

"Sometimes," I said, "you have to learn how to redefine your goals on your way to accomplishing them."

I could not have known how soon I would have to follow my own advice.

It happened that weekend when my ITB band gave out during mile twenty of the Hartford Marathon. I had run the Chicago Marathon the year before and this time I was on pace to run an even better time. For those of you, who like me, do not understand medical terms, ITB stands for the Ilio Tibial Band in your knee. It is the muscle that makes your knee bend. Since my knee was no longer bending, I made up my mind I would finish what I had started no matter what. Along the route people kept urging me to give up. "You might as well quit, you won't cross the finish in time to get your medal!"

I shouted back "No way! My determination is stronger than my knee!"

Around mile twenty-two, I met a young man who had an unfortunate run-in with a pothole at mile ten and blew out his knee as well. He was sixteen years old, and this was his first marathon. His shoes were falling apart, and not a single person from his family was there to cheer him on. To make matters worse, he had a two hour drive home ahead of him and would have to clutch his standard shift with the bad leg! He had redefined his goal and planned to finish the last sixteen of the twenty-six mile race with one good leg. We talked as we both limped our way through the last four miles. I told him that I had run the Chicago Marathon a year earlier — and when you are not injured and cross that finish line with the crowds cheering and your very last bit of adrenaline pouring forth, the sense of accomplishment is indescribable. I urged him to run again someday when his knee healed. I learned that his name was Michael, he was home schooled, and had trained to run thirty miles. The longest distance I had trained for was eighteen. Since I had been competing at Miss America prior to this particular race, I had not trained much — thus the injury. When I offered him some pain reliever, he politely declined. His family did not take medicine under any circumstances.

Michael and I finished the race seven minutes before they closed the gate; I grabbed his hand as we limped across the finish line. There was no final sprint, and there were no crowds cheering us on; just my fiance, and a few friends who had completed the run hours before and were waiting for me. We were not super-heroes and we did not run a race in record time. We had readjusted our goals in order to obtain a sense of accomplishment and won a medal for finishing. I told the kids at my next school appearance the story, and how in many ways that medal (I passed it around for them to see) meant more to me than any other.

After that weekend, I thought that the lesson I learned in the run had a strong application to the aftermath of the 9/11 crisis I was part of at Atlantic City.

I had set out for this event like any other young woman across the country fortunate enough to be blessed with the opportunity to compete for the title of Miss America. I was anxious, excited, hopeful and of course, exhausted, from months of hard work and preparation. I went there with very high expectations of myself, and a goal to make the top ten.

I was talking with Miss Arkansas, Jessie Ward, while we awaited our costume fittings, when we heard that a plane had hit one of the World Trade Center Towers. Thinking, like many others, that a small Cessna or similar plane had accidentally collided with the tall building, we passed it off until the director of security for the Miss American organization came running into the dressing room with a small, ancient looking radio, and we learned the worst. A second plane had hit the other tower. When he finally told us that they were both commercial 737s, the dead silence was broken with gasps and sobs. From there we huddled around the radio and listened as the Pentagon was hit, and it seemed the entire world was coming to an end. Instantly, I thought of how school children felt during World War I and II, listening to a radio's tales of destruction, waiting to duck under a desk for refuge at a moments notice. We were unable to see a television report and fully grasp the enormity of the devastation until late that afternoon.

There was much discussion among the contestants whether or not the show should go on. As you know, it did, but not without much debate and deliberation. I think at that deciding moment, we all redefined our goals a little bit. Suddenly, the temptation to run home to the safety of New Hampshire, and the comforting warmth of friends and family was overcome by a sense of patriotism. Patriotism, which I believe for most of us, was innate. The spirit of competition was no longer there for me, and was replaced with the indefatigable spirit of a nation.

I always said that because of my intense sense of patriotism and desire to entertain, I would have made a great USO woman. The opportunity did not present itself to me and I would not be boosting the spirits of service men and women overseas. Instead, I would be boosting the morale of my country and my home through the magic of national television.

I did not go on to make the top ten, nor the top twenty for that matter, but I had redefined a goal and brought it to fruition. The night of Miss America, I knew deep in my heart, I had joined forces with fifty other women from across the United States to show that we are all together and no one can stop us. For any young woman in the Miss America Organization, or any person in any leadership position, it is important to lead by example. Do not give up. Redefine. Reflect. And move on. We can all do great things.

Miss New Jersey 2001

Julie Barber

Heartbreak and Recovery

*T*he red beads on my gown glimmered and shimmered and playfully reflected the spotlight as once again I told my well-rehearsed story of the drama-filled events of Miss America 2001. As I listened to myself recite this tale at a local pageant, the crown of Miss New Jersey grew heavier on my head, and I felt like a bit of a phony. The words I spoke were true; every detail was how I remembered it. But my real story of triumph in the midst of tragedy is more complex, more humbling. I do love telling people about the solidarity and friendship that developed among the Miss America contestants after September 11, and how our resolve was steeled to go out and do good. It is a story the public should hear. It is true. But for me, those days in Atlantic City were only the beginning of my journey.

September 23, 2001 found me back in my home town after two and a half weeks of Miss America frenzy. It was the Sunday after I placed in the bottom thirty-one at the national competition, and I was attending mass with my parents. As the priest began the ceremony, I was caught up on all that had occurred nationally and to me personally since the last time I attended service. While at the Miss America Pageant, I was so intent on remaining calm, I had not allowed myself to grieve or even really process what had taken place, and silently, I began to cry. The more I thought about the families torn apart, the orphaned children, and the fallen heroes in New York, Washington D.C. and in the airplanes, the more piercingly I felt my own loss. I, too, felt robbed of my future.

After all, I did not go to Miss America competition to lose. As my crying deepened, guilt rose in me. How could I, kneeling in the house of God, equate my loss with the nightmare of September 11? I had no right. Still the tears came as my misery, confusion and questioning continued throughout mass. Finally, my mother noticed my crying. I tried to wipe away the tears, but it was too late. She began to tear up. That is when I knew I had to stop. I had to be strong.

For weeks I was consumed with misery and kept busy with the task of hiding it from loved ones. I spent hours in my car alone; went to bed at eight o'clock in the evening; made excuses for not being able to see my friends. In October I even broke up with my boyfriend because I was deeply ashamed at how bad I still felt.

By November, my moods were unpredictable. I was happy to finally be doing some work as Miss New Jersey, promoting mental health awareness. It was extremely rewarding to reach out to children and bring them some light in the darkness. However, each uplifting time was offset by periods of hopelessness, self-pity and anger. I was an ugly person for two months.

Resentment built as Thanksgiving drew closer. I was informed that I had to spend my favorite childhood holiday smiling and waving in a parade outside in another state. I would miss the Rockettes usher in Santa, and the rivalrous home town football games. Instead I would be freezing my booties off with Miss Pennsylvania, Miss Delaware and Miss America. At first I thought it would be fun to hang out with Katie Harman, and we could find out what it is like to be Miss America. I figured we could all have dinner together the night before and maybe slumber-party the night away. However, Miss America was unable to attend dinner, so it was just Misses Pennsylvania, Delaware and I.

I have to admit it was refreshing to spend time with Rosalyn and Erin. They helped to calm me down a bit, and I ended up having a wonderful time. Still, when I settled in for the night on my Holiday Inn bed and thought about Miss America at the Four Seasons, some of my resentment returned. I loved Katie, so I was never upset that she won. Instead, I was angry mostly at fate for convincing me that I would be Miss America, bringing me so close to that goal, yet ultimately leaving me so far out in the cold. (As I stood on stage watching Katie being crowned, it was a nightmare. I cannot count the times I envisioned that moment for me.) Lying in bed Thanksgiving Eve, as I felt bitterness course through my veins, I struggled to laugh again at the jokes Rosalyn, Erin and I had shared at dinner. I drifted off to sleep praying that God would truly give me a heart full of gratitude.

And it worked.

As I labored to write this story, I had the most trouble with this section. I knew that on Thanksgiving a magical transformation took place. But how to accurately describe it? I could not pinpoint the moment when this epiphany took place. Was it something insightful Rosalyn or Erin said to me? Was it the first sight of Katie on Thanksgiving morning when I seemed to become an anxious nine-year-old girl in awe of Miss America? Was it when I stood on the float and looked down to see dozens of police officers keeping us safe in their quiet, efficient way? Maybe it was the military groups I saw, as I imagined the sacrifices they have made time and time again for our nation.

I cannot tell you one exact image that clinched it for me that day. I just know that after Thanksgiving 2001, I lived my life differently. I was more committed to service and gratitude and I was in awe of creation. I felt like I was a part of living history as I rode through the streets of the magnificent town where our country was born, and we made a collective statement of resiliency. I remember watching and listening in captured, contented amazement as *God Bless America* rang from Katie's magnificent, pure voice. I remember feeling like I was a valuable part of all that was going on around me — I was a vital link in every family, every Boy Scout and police officer lining the street. Thanksgiving Day I saw once again how much we all have to be grateful. I could not believe how many blessings I had forgotten or undervalued in the past months. I made it my mission that day to never forget those blessings and to pass them on to others.

My understanding also reinforced the value of my platform to raise public awareness of teenage mental issues. As a result of 9/11, so many more have needed counseling this year to help them deal with daily struggles and often puzzling emotions. Children especially have experienced feelings of great anxiety and fear.

With a 30,000-dollar grant from Saint Clare's Behavioral Health Services, I was able to reach out to these frightened children, and help them to connect with the services they needed. I have worked with the Mental Health Association of Southwestern New Jersey to raise awareness of teenage mental health problems, such as eating disorders, depression and suicide. I have talked to state legislators, educators, parents and business people throughout my state to increase awareness and funding for mental health.

Most importantly, my inner turmoil and triumph in the shadow of September 11, have taught me that the greatest fundamental of American attributes is an endless potential for growth and improvement. I tell people that a Miss America is inside each one of us, no matter what race, religion, age or even gender we are. When we believe in limitless possibilities and work toward improving ourselves every day, true success is ours.

May all Americans take heart in this quintessentially American dream.

Miss New Mexico
2001

Marta
Strzyzewski

Only in America

*I*n the year of 1984, at the age of six, I immigrated to the United States from Poland. The communist government in Poland was oppressive, and there was economic hardship.

My father was part of the Solidarity Movement, a group which resisted the communist government. Just before martial law was declared, my father, fearing for his family and for his own life, escaped to America. The United States granted him political asylum in 1982. Two years later, my mother, baby brother and I joined him in America. This is where my story begins.

Coming from a communistic country, I greatly appreciate the freedoms that America offers. These same freedoms are available even to the newcomers who are not yet citizens of this great country. The inalienable rights of life, liberty and the pursuit of happiness are qualities that everyone enjoys.

At a young age I learned that America is bursting with countless opportunities for everyone, and that with hard work, dedication and perseverance, people can meet their goals and make their dreams come true. I became a United States citizen when I was fourteen.

So many people were so gracious and generous to my family when we first set foot onto the "Land of the Free". It was my turn to give back to the community and I chose to work with immigrants and refugees who had the same dream as I did. I am a volunteer worker with the Catholic Charities of Central New Mexico's Refugee Resettlement Program. I was able to help people from other countries feel welcome. I also volunteered with Senator Jeff Bingaman to work on immigration and naturalization issues.

When it came to choosing a platform for the Miss America program, my choice was clear. It became "Let Freedom Ring: Establish U.S. Citizenship".

I was in a dressing room with three other Miss America contestants, trying on production number outfits, when I heard the news: "A plane flew into one of the World Trade Center's Twin Towers!"

The happy faces I had seen just a few minutes earlier were now filled with tears and fear. The happy chatter and the laughter died. The dressing room was as silent as a tomb.

The news made me scared and upset at first. Then anger crept in. Who did this? Who would ever attack our great country? It seemed that it took only a couple of hours to find out the answer: It was the shameful work of terrorists. The news broadcasters even announced where the terrorists were from, and the organization with which they were affiliated. We had no way of seeing what happened, so we asked Miss America organizers to bring us a television set. For three hours most of us sat on the hard, cold, wooden floor, some of the other girls were seated in metal chairs — all watching the terrifying images on the television in shock as the scenes of attack kept replaying.

Every day from then on, we prayed. We prayed in a big circle together as a group. The praying helped to fill the hole in my heart. But I still had a strange, stomach-turning feeling about my platform. I wanted to help people become United States citizens, especially at a moment when our country had lost trust in foreigners. We did not know whom to believe; even the

Immigration and Naturalization Service was under close scrutiny. It seemed that we had been careless about letting foreigners into our free land. Should we be stricter on our immigration policies? I was asking these questions of myself. In a time of national crisis, I had to re-analyze my own thoughts and beliefs.

After days of thinking, I realized a few things. About one million immigrants arrive in the United States each year. Undocumented immigrants constitute one percent of the total United States population. And six out of ten illegal immigrants enter the United States legally with a student, tourist or business visa, and end up staying when the visa expires. There are countless people who want to come and live in our country. We cannot, physically keep everybody out. Also, it became clear that a person who desperately wants the freedom and opportunities that this country has to offer, and has the courage to immigrate, is most likely going to be an asset to America.

We do have the obligation to scrutinize those who come in, and be on guard against those who would do us harm. But the more significant question raised by the statistics concerning immigrants is: "Why are immigrants staying in America instead of going back home to the countries of their origin?" The answer is obvious: This *is* the land of the free. And, without fail, those who have experienced freedom will fight to preserve it for themselves and others.

We have all been transplanted from other places on the globe. The Statue of Liberty beckons to ...*the poor and huddled masses* ... ready to embrace the new arrivals to America. It is our tradition, and we should keep our arms and hearts open to others who wish to share our good fortune.

Miss New York 2001

Andrea Plummer

The City That Never Sleeps

"*I* *n the long history of the world, only a few generations have been granted the role of defending freedom in its hour of maximum danger. I do not shrink from this responsibility ... I welcome it.*"

These inspiring words by John F. Kennedy echo the feelings I had while serving as Miss New York. When I first won that title in June of 2001, I never anticipated the hurdles that I would have to overcome or the challenges I would face during my year. Then again, how could anyone have foreseen what would happen on September 11, 2001?

A half an hour later, as I arrived at the Atlantic City Convention Hall, I knew immediately that my Miss America experience would be unlike any other. With the attacks on the World Trade Center's Twin Towers devastating my own city and state, all eyes turned on me. The other contestants and volunteers wanted to know how I was taking the news.

Did I know someone working in the towers? How was I going to handle everything now? Thrown into a role I had never envisioned for myself, I knew I needed to be strong for the other contestants, and help decide whether to go on or not. While I put up a courageous front, I spent hours in my hotel room at night crying for those lost, and for those friends of mine whom I could not reach. When finally I heard that my friends and family were safe, I pressed forward with renewed strength.

President Bush gave a speech during the week that encouraged us to carry on and celebrate the freedoms we have as Americans. His words inspired me to remain firm so that our nation would know that fear was not going to win.

When I stood on the Miss America stage on September 22nd and introduced myself as Miss New York, I was filled with an overwhelming sense of pride and honor, for during the week since the attacks, the people of New York had not allowed terrorism to change or divide them. Rather they had bonded together, serving as a beacon of strength and hope for the rest of the nation.

The day I returned to New York City, I was shocked to find a city that resembled a ghost town rather than the ... *city that never sleeps.* There was a strange, perhaps even sad, aura about the normally bustling streets, now devoid of any visitors.

New York! My New York! The heartbeat of the nation, the place where music, dance and theatre are born, where color, races, nationalities blend to make it a fabulous place of excitement and discovery, always ready to welcome the world. Oh, I know, we will come back. You just can't keep New Yorkers down for long, or for that matter, the rest of our great nation. But for a while, we'll mourn the loss of lives as we look at the hideous scars the cowardly terrorist attack left at Ground Zero.

The reality of what occurred slowly began to sink in. The truth became clearer when I visited the 85th Street Fire Station which had lost more than ten firemen. From the survivors I heard stories about the events of that unforgettable day. As the men shared their grief with me, the alarm bell sounded, and they were out of the door within minutes.

I was taken with the passion of their steadfast commitment. I thought that if they can keep going despite their terrible losses, so can the rest of this city. It was in that moment that my true purpose as Miss New York unfolded. It was my job to spread awareness of Multiple Sclerosis, my original platform, but more importantly, I had to encourage the people of New York state to press on, and keep their commitment to their causes, their businesses and their families. I decided to utilize my position as a Lieutenant in the United States Air Force Reserves to inspire people to support our great country.

At each appearance, I offered hope and encouragement. While the war on terrorism was taking place in Afghanistan, I fought to keep the spirits high here in New York. I walked on stage during a USO show in Brooklyn wearing my Air Force uniform and told the troops the story of my Miss America experience. As I performed a dance to *Merry Christmas Darling* for them, I thought how rewarding it was to be entertaining the servicemen with whom one day I may be standing side by side, fulfilling my active duty commitment after I finish medical school.

As I look back on my year as Miss New York, I never think of the crown or competition. It was never about winning the crown. I think of the excitement on the children's faces who learned the Pledge of Allegiance in sign language, and the sparkle in the eyes of the child who saluted me in my uniform.

I think of a city that went from being stunned into mournful silence to once again making its mark, as the thriving, bustling, all-alive Big Apple.

I know now why I was chosen to be Miss New York 2001. God knew that I would not back down when our American spirit was attacked. My faith in Him and my love for America carried me over each obstacle that I faced.

As John F. Kennedy said, "very few are called to defend this nation's freedom." I am grateful to have been one of them.

Miss North Carolina 2001

Ashley Nicole House

Hope, Courage and Hard work

*W*ith so many fond memories from my year of service, traveling from the Atlantic seashore to the Smokey mountains, it is difficult to choose which recollections to share. However, my first "official appearance" as Miss North Carolina at the Southport Fourth of July Celebration was memorable. During the parade, a shirtless spectator decided to hitch a ride on my parade vehicle. He was what I like to call a "good old country boy." With a beer in his hand, wearing only shorts, sandals, and a pair of mirrored sunglasses and big huge belly exposed for the entire world to see, he jumped on the back of my convertible and rode approximately two blocks with me down the parade route. The smell of alcohol was enough to frighten any woman or light a torch. As he moved within inches of my face, he slid his sunglasses to the end of his nose and said, "Ma'am, you got purty eyes." How about that for a southern gentleman?

Little did any of us know how much we really should be celebrating our independence. Only months later our freedom would be compromised, and no July 4th celebration would ever be the same again.

Not only did our nation change on September 11, 2001, so did the job of Miss North Carolina. I did not realize how much, until I appeared at the Mullet Festival exactly one month after the attacks. When I arrived in Swansboro, North Carolina, I was to be greeted by two marines who were to escort me for the remainder of the weekend. I knew that it was my responsibility to keep things light hearted and fun for them over the next two days, because the terrible reality of terrorism awaited their return. After the introductions were made and we discussed where we were from, one of the marines asked me what a mullet was, and what the festival was all about. My response was that I did not know, since the only mullet I every heard of was the haircut! To our relief, a mullet is actually a fish and the festival was celebrating its impact on North Carolina's fishing industry. That evening we began discussing what it is like to be in the Marine Corp and what their jobs entailed. Of course, September 11 came up. While a lot of information was classified, I did get some insight on how it had affected their lives so far. Never in my life have I been moved as I was by how they described their love, devotion and patriotism for their country.

Over the course of the weekend, I noticed crowd participation and enthusiasm had drastically changed from previous festivals I had attended. However, when I walked in escorted by two Marines, people stood and applauded, and I could see the pride reflected in their eyes. I thought the applause was for the Marines because they really deserved it. But I was wrong! People thanked me for being there and for going on in spite of what had happened. I have never forgotten the words a lady on the Mullet Festival committee said to me, "You are such a blessing to North Carolina because we really need you right now. Thank you for being here." It was then that I was presented with a key to the city.

On November 7th, 2001, I received a letter from Beverly Perdue, the lieutenant governor of North Carolina. She wrote, "Our state is better because of the leadership you provide to build a better North Carolina."

Many such letters from various organizations followed in the months after the attack. One letter was from Jenny Foster, Director of Development for the Ronald McDonald House in Chapel Hill, North Carolina. She said, "To actively see how members of our community and beyond provide for us day in, and day out means more to them than you could ever possibly imagine during what is the most difficult, stressful, and challenging time of their lives. The children were absolutely gaga over you (and chattered incessantly after you left), but the adults were exceptionally charmed by your attentiveness and inherent sweetness. My mom drove down from Roanoke to volunteer for the day, and couldn't stop talking about what a sweet young lady you were — you made quite an impression."

The message I carried as Miss North Carolina was one of hope, courage, love, determination, and hard work. Looking back over my reign, I see that I have grown in more ways than I ever thought possible. My patriotism, not only for my country, but also for me has grown. I have never in my life been more proud to be a southerner from North Carolina! The kindness, support, generosity, and hospitality I have experienced this year have truly warmed my heart.

With each new friendship, smile, handshake and laughter shared, I was constantly reminded of the honor bestowed upon me. That is the reason that I love calling North Carolina home.

Miss North Dakota 2001

Jillayne Mertens

A Gift of Life

*A*ll my life, I have been a jock, a basketball and volleyball star. Contestants for pageants, I thought, were girls really stuck on themselves. When I entered the Miss North Dakota pageant, I was focused primarily on scholarship money. When I won and was on my way to Miss America I did not have charitable thoughts about what the other women would be like. Boy, was I wrong. Never had I been with a group of such beautiful, smart, sweet, nice, wonderful, women. Each one had such a great story to tell, sharing the experiences that molded her into an outstanding person. I would like to share some of my experiences with them.

After the shock of the attacks on America, I realized, as the other women did, that we would act as messengers of courage to Americans in every state — a new role for each of us. As I returned home to take up my tasks, I recalled my teenage years which were not all that easy. My mother was diagnosed with leukemia at age

127

fourteen. This led me inevitably to my platform issue which is the National Marrow Donor Program (NMDP). She was fortunate to find a perfect donor match which saved her life.

Everyone in our family is aware of how lucky my mom was, but it still hurts all of us to know of the many people who entered the hospital the same day as she, did not get a match and did not survive. In a way, that makes us feel guilty.

I cannot keep thinking that if every person reading my story were a member of the bone marrow registry, everybody in need of a match would be able to receive a life-giving gift.

If you are over the age of eighteen and under the age of sixty, you could save a life of someone who is in need. Isn't that amazing? You could experience the gift of giving while you are alive. Bless those who have already given to the NMDP registry, and I pray for those who continue to battle blood diseases. Throughout my year of service, I have met many people who have cancer. I was touched by a little boy who had Phanconia leukemia. His name is Dylan Dilaney; he is nine years old and faces the nightmare of a rare bone disease. Because he is so young and the disease is so rare, finding the right donor will be hard for him. You may be the person who can save his life. So, let us get educated, give your bone marrow and save a life. All you have to do is call 1-800-marrow-2 and get the information you need on how to get started.

It has been an exciting year for me, especially because of the response I have received from thousands of school children. I would like to make a suggestion for anyone who feels lost in his or her world: follow your heart and have faith in yourself. I would have never been at Miss America if I had not believed in myself. And even when life throws you a curve, pick yourself up and there will be a better tomorrow. Respect yourself and others. This will lead you to many good friendships and lasting connections. And create your future. Whatever that may be.

God truly blessed me by making it possible for me to meet fifty other young women of courage, determination and love of country. Now everlasting friends, we are sisters forever. Bless Katie Harman for taking on such great leadership after September 11. We all love you and pray for you. Thank you for representing us so well. Thanks to the Miss America organization for helping women change their lives forever.

I am so glad I am part of it all.

*Miss Ohio
2001*

*Natalie Elizabeth
Witwer*

Love Is Spelled G-I-V-E

*W*hen I considered competing for the Miss Ohio title, I just wasn't too sure about it — beauty pageants didn't impress me. What I value can't be found on the outside in the form of a crown or a pretty dress. It comes from who I am according to my heart. When I was twelve years old, I gave my life to God and said — take all of it, run with it, and I'll follow. It was that commitment that carried me to where I am today. I promised God that I would run for Miss Ohio for Him — not for me.

I took a firm stand for Youth Ministry and for my faith. When my name was announced as the Miss Ohio winner, I was surprised because I never expected it to happen. I wasn't sure I had the qualifications to be Miss Ohio. I wanted to wait until I was older. However, some of the greatest moments in life happen when you least expect them. I love the saying, "God doesn't always call the equipped, but He equips the called."

I have grown and learned so much this year with each new experience. Winning Miss Ohio, and being involved in the Miss America Scholarship Program is not simply a destination, but the beginning of a journey. It is preparation for the future because I have been motivated to have my own ministry — to develop, write, think, and pray so that I can be effective.

Traveling 40,000 miles across Ohio, I have learned to communicate my platform of Youth Ministry with the words from Matthew 5:14-16: *You are the light of the world. A city on a hill cannot be hidden. Neither do people light a lamp and put it under a bowl. Instead they put it on its stand, and it gives light to everyone in the house. In the same way, let your light shine before men, that they may see your good deeds and praise your Father in heaven.*

I encourage kids to be a light for the world daily — to dig deep and face their lives in a real way. Life isn't meant to be mundane, I tell them. It's meant to be lived as an adventure. Encompassing all of this, my motto is: "Let your Heart Shine from the Inside, Out!"

I remember the Miss America Pageant as though I'm watching a documentary on television. As tragic information came pouring out of a radio in the dressing room, we huddled together listening to the terrible news — devastated and shocked. Some of us responded by covering our faces, some of us cried, some fell into silence, some sought hugs from others and some turned to prayer. Life has a way of taking us up and taking us down again. It's hard, isn't it? And a lot of times we don't know quite what to think.

When I am puzzled as I was then, I think of Ecclesiastes, Verse 8:17: *Then I saw all that God has done. No one can comprehend what goes on under the sun. Despite all his efforts to search it out, man cannot discover its meaning.*

So then what? We must walk by faith. And as I walk, I search for knowledge and wisdom and understanding. A lot of times we learn so much more when we suffer, because it forces us to face life's difficulties. Suffering breaks us down and leads us to find a way to get back up again. Many of us have experienced sorrow, only to have bounced back to move forward with confidence that

God is working through all of these things to shape us to be the best we can be.

Being Miss Ohio, has made me understand that we are put in certain places for definite reasons. As I meet people from different places and diverse backgrounds, I am certain that this life is about touching others with love — even if it's just a warm smile or a whisper that says, "Your life counts."

Being Miss Ohio I learned, has been about serving and helping other people. The word "love" is spelled "G-I-V-E" in my book, and that was my purpose as Miss Ohio.

Miss Oklahoma 2001

Kaci Hundley

Icing on the Cake

*P*eople always ask me what my experience competing for the Miss America title was like, and I tell them that it was unlike anything any former Miss Oklahoma could ever imagine. Being Miss Oklahoma was an honor I had always dreamed of while I was growing up. I have never forgotten watching the Miss Oklahoma ceremonies, and I longed for the day when I would have my chance.

Winning a state title brings opportunities of a lifetime and the obligation and opportunity to make a difference in the lives of the people where you live. Competing for the Miss America title was the icing on the cake for me. Having that dream come true was simply unbelievable. I remember pulling into Atlantic city on the train to the welcome of a cheering crowd and the notes of the famous Miss America song, *There She Is …* filling the air. Sometimes I still have to pinch myself that I was actually there.

Tuesday morning, September 11, I was in the first group of contestants that arrived at the convention center for fitting costumes we were to wear in the production number for the telecast. We were all sitting in the dressing room when a panicked security officer ran in shouting the news of the attacks. With no access to telephone or television, we could not begin to imagine what was happening. We finally found a small radio and we sat transfixed in horror as we listened to the tragedy our country was facing. I could not believe what I was hearing. Our nation, the greatest and strongest one in the world, was under attack from some misguided terrorists. How ironic that we were at the Miss America pageant during our country's most difficult hour. What now?

My initial reaction, like the other women, was to go home. I just wanted to be in the comfort of my own state with my family. I almost felt guilty competing in a scholarship pageant when our nation was going through such misery. I was not sure having the Miss America Pageant go on was the appropriate thing to do. But after much thought and prayer, I realized that having the pageant was a way to signify our courage and strength. After a week and a half of mourning, our country was going to be ready to begin its healing process. What better way than to uplift the spirit of our countrymen with the colorful, upbeat and traditional Miss America Pageant. I began to realize that my reason for being there was far greater than just to compete.

The experience changed the meaning of Miss Oklahoma for me. Earlier, I had thought nothing could be worse than what we Oklahoman's went through on April 19, 1995 when the terrible Oklahoma City bombing shattered an institution and many innocent lives. I knew that if Oklahoma could pull together and recover as it did, our nation would do no less and would overcome and respond with a firm will.

I will never look at the American flag in the same way, or think about Miss America without remembering the deep bond we fifty-one women created. We went through a time together that no one would ever understand. The emotions, pressures, fears, and uncertainties that we felt are indescribable and only known by the "Class of 2001." We needed each other's strength and comfort. The feeling of going on national television in a common spirit of unity to do something for a nation in need of healing, was a feeling that only we women of Miss America Pageant 2001 can understand.

Since I returned to my state, I have had the opportunity to perform at many American rallies. It has been a blessing to be an ambassador for Oklahoma at a time in history when people required reassurance, hope, encouragement, leadership, and faith. To be able to share my Miss America story with the people of Oklahoma has been a high honor, and I truly believe that people now view the Miss America organization in a different light — much more than just a pageant. We are not just "pageant girls" or even celebrities, but simply real young women with strength, courage, and intelligence, determined to make a difference in the lives of people everywhere.

It is interesting and almost uncanny, that before going to Atlantic city, I looked up the scripture Esther 4:14. It reads: *"... and who knows but that you have been called to royal position for such a time as this."*

When I arrived at the Miss America competition, I discovered that almost every contestant had found that scripture and had taken it to heart. God was preparing us for the challenge of our lives: a challenge that would require us to give hope and restore faith to the people of our great nation. We were called to royal position for this time, and I am proud of the way we represented our nation, our states, and our faith.

Miss Oregon 2001

Katie Harman

An Ambassador of Hope

*O*ne crisp February day in Portland, Oregon, I sat down for tea and conversation with a woman who would forever change my life. As I looked into Christie's deep, knowing eyes and felt the impact of her honest insight into her advanced breast cancer diagnosis, I sensed a calling in my soul — a calling to make Christie's feelings and thoughts about the disease that had ravaged her entire body known to all who would listen.

She spoke of her love for the sun when it poured through the atrium which her husband had built for her, as well as her daily quest for a quality life. She shared the story of meeting her husband and of his unending support. We laughed at crazy memories of past family vacations. We wiped away tears when we talked about the horrors of breast cancer. She described her treatments and therapies and spoke of her trust in her oncologist. We briefly touched on the transition from life to death, and she boldly spoke of her desire to live life to the fullest.

At one point in our conversation, Christie set her teacup down on a nearby table, turned her steady gaze directly on me, and proclaimed, "We need you, Katie. Those of us with breast cancer need you to communicate the importance of quality of life and hope, to give us a voice."

On September 11, 2001, at nine o' clock at night, I sat on the edge of my bed in my hotel room in Atlantic City, New Jersey, with my head cradled in my hands and Christie's call to action in my thoughts. The lives of every American citizen had changed that day and I was trying to digest the horrors of the situation, as well as uncover my purpose for competing in the 2001 Miss America Pageant during such a time. Earlier that evening on the telephone, I had shared my fears and thoughts with my parents and the executive directors of the Miss Oregon Scholarship Program, Dana and Steve Phillips — whom I considered my second set of parents. Amidst our prayers, tears, and reflections, a revelation unfolded: the path to discover hope and life that breast cancer patients journeyed every day, was also the need of the American people at that time.

When I lifted my head from my hands, I knew deep in my heart that my purpose as Miss Oregon 2001 or as Miss America 2002, was to take Christie's request to a new level and communicate hope and quality of life to a nation with many breast cancer patients — fathers, mothers, students, laborers, legislators, professionals, children and so many more who needed to experience life in the midst of death.

When I was indeed blessed with the opportunity to serve as Miss America 2002, I discovered more about the true nature of hope than I had ever imagined possible. My travels have taken me into the lives of courageous, determined, compassionate individuals and given me the chance to draw wisdom and understanding from the experiences that we shared.

I learned it from the ash-covered rescue workers at Ground Zero committed to aid this country with their blood, sweat and tears, to the brave men and women of the armed forces assisting family members of the victims of the Pentagon attack with compassion and strength. The children representing Children's Miracle Network Hospitals across the nation with smiles as bright as the sun and joy emanating from every fiber of their being were others, as were the several thousand women and hundreds of men who have lived with or are currently battling breast cancer. Their desire to share with others the hope that motivates them to value every moment of every day was uplifting. Nor can I ever forget the countless others who have proven what can be accomplished with sheer determination and high aspirations.

The American Heritage Dictionary defines hope as "a wish or desire accompanied by confident expectation of its fulfillment." I define hope as an opportunity to grasp hold of the true beauty of life and share with others its radiance. As I reflect upon my quest to encourage the nation, I find that I was in turn also comforted and inspired by the very people whom I desired to serve. I now truly believe that the spirit of America flows forth from the hope that its citizens harbor in their hearts.

During my second week as Miss America, this faith was solidified after I viewed the exhibit of the "Star Spangled Banner" at the Smithsonian Institution — the original flag from 1812 that inspired Francis Scott Key to write what would become the nation's anthem. When I looked closely at this tattered, but magnificent flag, I noticed something about the precious symbol that I had taken for granted in times past.

I realized that the strength of the flag relied upon the tiny stitches that bound together its three different colors and shapes. Even though each stitch was its own individual entity, the formation of those stitches into a beautiful and inspiring flag made a tremendous impact on me, evoking pride, respect, and a sense of unity.

We as Americans are like stitches. We are of different races, religions, or creeds. We have differing motivations and dreams. We are from diverse cultures and environments. We have different personalities and levels of understanding. But when we bond together with hope and the common goal of quality of life for all Americans, we are able to produce pride, respect and unity — further enriching our lives and filling our souls with peace.

As stitches unite the flag, the contribution of each individual citizen unites and strengthens our nation. A new awareness that we are one, as citizens of America, if we work together on behalf of each other and for all. This unifying message has come forth from the terrible tragedies of September 11. May we all answer this new call to service, and together see the fruits that a cooperative effort can bring forth.

Christie's request and vision continue to ring loudly in my mind — more so now when tragedy combined with experiences that I have had. I am deeply grateful that her words have set a course for my life. Just as America will never be the same after this historic year, this Miss America will never be the same either. I will devote my life to being an ambassador of hope.

Miss Pennsylvania 2001

Rosalyn Menon

Goals, Plans and Good Intentions

*I*n the heartland of my state, lies the heart of America. Here, fallen heroes found their final, hard-won resting place, in a little town called Shanksville. Along with the rest of the world, I watched in one part amazement, one part horror, as the details of the last hijacked plane of September 11, 2001 came to light. I listened to the privileged, intimate, final last words of a husband to his wife. And I felt the reverberations of the most important and difficult day of my generation's life, as the terror began to affect not only my nation, but also my own home turf.

From the instant the fifty other contestants and I began listening on a hastily found radio to the events of 9/11 as they unfolded, I understood that all of my new sisters and I were about to embark on an entirely new journey. We came to represent our states at the Miss America Pageant with aspirations and goals, with plans and good intentions. All of these were altered after the attacks on our country.

Now, we would return home with the responsibility of lifting the morale of our fellow citizens.

As I began my travels around my state, from Erie to Philadelphia, from the north to the south, and from the smallest boroughs to our most metropolitan areas, I knew deeply and truly 9/11 affected every person I met.

I think that particularly for my generation, 9/11 will be our day "that will live in infamy." Every person has his or her own story of where they were, how they heard, and who they knew directly affected by the suicidal terrorists. But perhaps more importantly, my past year as Miss Pennsylvania taught me, more than ever, that people should live their lives to the fullest.

I continue to be amazed at how strongly people have been moved by the heroism and sacrifices of others.

As Miss Pennsylvania, one of the most memorable appearances I had the privilege of attending this year, was a "Thank-You" weekend, honoring members of the fire department of New York with a getaway vacation in Philadelphia. I served as the hostess of the weekend, personally representing Philadelphia, and all of Pennsylvania, in our gratitude for the heroism and hard work these firefighters displayed. We had a memorable weekend of motorcade travel in stretch limousines, VIP seating at concerts and sporting events, fine dining at some of Philadelphia's renowned eating establishments. Our representatives of the FDNY were given significant donations to help fund numerous fire fighter charities. Most importantly, at parades and fund raising events, our New York City heroes won the adoration and applause of Pennsylvanians. But for me personally, I was given a glimpse into the real lives of these brave men whom I admired, but knew little about. They received heart-felt thanks, through handshakes, hugs, and many tears of gratitude.

I learned about their unions, their hopes, and their fears. I met their families, friends, and relatives. And I heard first hand, over dinner, or before the start of a concert, their own traumatic stories.

One man was named Freddie. Freddie is handsome, my age, full of zest and zeal. He loves good music, having fun with his friends, and his job as a fireman. He always knew he was going to be a firefighter. He wanted to follow in his father's footsteps. On September 11, Freddie not only followed in his father's footsteps, but began the daunting task of filling in his vacant shoes. Freddie, like many others, lost his father in the collapse of the World Trade Center. I wondered if he questioned his choice to be a firefighter, whether he was angry that his father's profession led him to his death. But Freddie is strong and knew what his father would have answered: He loved his job and died doing what he loved — helping others.

Before we know it, it will be a year since the events of September 11, 2001. A few days ago, I attended the memorial service for a friend's father whose body was never recovered from the World Trade Center. The service was beautiful, filled with hope and laughter. Rather than focusing on the unfair death of my friend's father, we celebrated his life. I looked at the pictures of him displayed near the symbolically empty casket. His smile, the pride in his eyes as he danced with his daughter at her wedding. The joy of holding a grandchild. The excitement of cutting a birthday cake. These snippets of his life live on in his family and friends.

When former New York Mayor Giuliani spoke at the high school graduation ceremony in the small town of Shanksville, Pennsylvania, I was struck with the true meaning of commencement. It meant not an end, but a moving on, a starting anew. And, America has what it takes to do that.

Miss Rhode Island 2001

Jennifer D'Ambrosio

Making a Difference

I always knew I wanted to help people. I always knew that somehow I could make a difference in their lives. I was a child with many aspirations, and many adversities. My higher education would be difficult to attain given that my mother was a single parent and raised my brother and me by herself. I was also plagued with seizures from the age of six, which made a challenge of studying.

In high school, I played three varsity sports and participated in many extracurricular activities, including community service. By my senior year, I had received several scholarships and made the decision to attend Providence College, a private liberal arts school. By this time, I had worked on many political campaigns and interned for a United States Senator. The way I could help people, I decided, was through better government and chose political science as a major. It was in my second year of college that I discovered the Miss Rhode Island program. I hoped to win scholarship money, but ended up with much more than that.

Winning the crown as Miss Rhode Island was, my first elected office, well sort of.

The issue I chose for my year of service was children's literacy. I love working with kids, especially because they remind me so much of myself when I struggled in school. I was a little girl with problems in reading, relegated to the lowest reading group in elementary school. I felt embarrassed to read in front of the class. I was fortunate though, because my mother took time to help me with my studies. She read to me and I read to her. Eventually, with extra work from my teacher, I was elevated to the highest reading group.

I have volunteered directly in schools, worked on literacy programs for the classroom, and recruited several people to become volunteers. I spoke throughout Rhode Island not only on children's literacy but on various issues and truly believe that I made a difference. Being from the smallest of states, I must admit it was not only difficult to prepare for Miss America, but quite challenging to keep up with the demand for appearances.

I was able to keep a part-time job during my year as Miss Rhode Island, and had two fund-raisers to help me on this journey. The program does not have many sponsors, and all the costs went to me, the titleholder. I remember spending ninety dollars of gas a week and finally realized that I could not afford my current schedule. I began to work out at the gym at my school and scheduled any meeting with the Rhode Island Board in the Providence area. In the end, my family and I spent much more than we expected. I did however end up with about $10,000 in scholarship money. But even with that, I still have outstanding school loans triple that amount.

The world of "pageants" was new to me, and I was nervous about going to the Miss America competition in September — the month our nation will never forget. As I met all of the state titleholders, I was surprised to learn that basically all of these young women were in Atlantic City for the same reason — the pursuit of their higher education by winning scholarship money. We were in high spirits and looked forward to the next two weeks. No one could have imagined that on our second day in Atlantic City our country would be attacked by terrorists.

Here we were representing all of the United States and we were rocked by hijacked planes that killed more people than the sneak attack on Pearl Harbor more than a half century earlier. I wanted to be with my family and my friends and flee from the Miss America Pageant. We learned about the toll of fatalities much later, but we knew then that we were part of an American tragedy.

Within a few days of the attacks, we had to decide if we wanted to go on with the pageant. I was one of the state titleholders who voted against going forward. I remember thinking that it was just too soon. My vote, as well as some other "no" votes were in the minority and we went on with the pageant. I know in my heart I was no longer bent on the competition. The group, however, focused on being strong for the nation. I am proud of all of us, especially because we were both physically and emotionally drained by the time of the September 22 Miss America television broadcast. We promised that the one who was blessed to be Miss America and who would represent all of us, be strong and reflect the determination of all the women who were there as examples of courage for all Americans. Katie Harman has done this job well and I am so proud of her.

Since giving up my crown in April, I have graduated from Providence College with a Bachelor of Arts degree in Political Science. I am taking a year off before starting graduate school and I'm currently applying to law schools. I know that I have helped make a difference working for literacy programs in the state of Rhode Island through my Miss America experience, and I sincerely hope to continue to make a difference in people's lives by running for political office someday. Another dream-come-true goal for me.

Miss South Carolina 2001

Jeanna Raney

Passionate Purpose

My dream of being crowned Miss South Carolina actually started when I was six years old. My parents took me to see the pageant in 1987, and like most little girls growing up in South Carolina, I too wanted to be queen of our state. However, in high school, I learned about the platform issue, the community service, and that the job of Miss South Carolina was not glamorous. I decided that I did *not* want to be Miss South Carolina after all. There was not an issue in my heart to which I was willing to dedicate my life for a year. Little did I know what God had in store for me.

My attitude completely changed as a freshman at the University of South Carolina when my mother committed suicide after suffering from the mental illness of depression. For a long time — most of my life — she battled many physical health problems that gave her a lot of pain, and eventually led to depression. She displayed all of the typical warning signs of a suicidal person, but my family and I blamed her symptoms on her medical problems. We had never been educated to recognize the warning signs that some suicidal persons display. When she died, my father and older brother, Jeremy, and I were in shock.

We had lost the person dearest to us and a heavy feeling of guilt kcpt us company. After learning more about the dangers of depression and suicide, it became obvious to us that mom had been teetering on the brink of suicide for a year. The night of the funeral, my father sat my brother and I down and said, "Jeremy and Jeanna, you both have a choice to make. You can either continue to feel sorry for yourselves, seek pity, and eventually become depressed just like your mom, or," he continued, "you can move on and learn from this terrible tragedy that we are going through."

It was not easy, but the three of us chose to move on, to learn, to accept, and be able to talk about what happened.

Soon after my mother died, I became an advocate for suicide prevention, whether I wanted to or not. I could have chosen another path, but I chose to help educate people about the warning signs leading to suicide. I knew that the position of Miss South Carolina would give me a statewide microphone to carry my message. That was the only reason I entered the pageant. My platform became the South Carolina National Alliance for the Mentally Ill, and the South Carolina Mental Health Association.

All the traditional items that Miss South Carolina receives are wonderful; the crown, $20,000 in scholarships, a wardrobe, jewelry, a cell phone, car washes, photo shoots, etc. All of those things are nice, but that is not the essence of Miss South Carolina.

To me, the true meaning of wearing the crown in my state, is defined by the fact that I have never given my speech without at least one person telling me how suicide has affected her or his life. The job often meant talking for hours to a teenage girl who did not want to tell her parents of her depression because she did not want to disappoint them.

It was about hearing from several psychiatrists that something in my speech could possibly help one of their patients. It was about having a Rotarian tell me that he had suffered from depression for more than ten years, and only after listening to me speak did he find the courage to talk about his illness.

I learned even more about my job after talking to a thirteen-year-old boy whose mother was dying of breast cancer. He told me that he wanted to commit suicide before she died, so that he would not have to deal with the pain of her death. My strength was renewed again when an eight-year-old girl whose father committed suicide told her aunt that she was "just like the queen," because she had something in common with Miss South Carolina. Ultimately, being Miss South Carolina was about having numerous people tell me that they were suicidal, but were now willing to seek treatment after hearing me speak. That is what being Miss South Carolina means to me.

When I left the Miss America Pageant to go back to my great state, I had no idea how desperately South Carolina needed a spokesperson for Mental Health issues, or how eagerly South Carolina would embrace my platform. I will always be an advocate for Suicide Prevention. I will always be an advocate for Mental Health issues. I will always share my mother's story so that other lives may be saved. Miss South Carolina was simply my launching pad. My passion and advocacy can only grow stronger as I continue to travel our country and share my message of hope.

That message is impassioned by my recollection of the fifty-one young women in Atlantic City who on September 11, decided that it would be our sign of defiance not to stop the Miss America pageant. We would not give the terrorists the satisfaction of having been responsible for derailing a time-honored American institution — a beloved tradition.

That morning I had an overwhelming feeling that if I was fortunate enough to become Miss America 2002, or if I went home as Miss South Carolina, I would be able to help people with the healing process of recovery, and ready to move on after the terrifying attacks on our country. I knew I could show people how to turn a "scar into a star" — turning a negative into a positive. No matter what the outcome of the 2001 Miss America Pageant, I was ready to do the job.

Miss South Dakota 2001

Alecia Ann Zuehlke

Perseverance + Tenacity = Success

*M*ine was a four-year journey, filled with ups and downs, to win the title of Miss South Dakota. I started competing in the Miss America system in 1997 as a freshman at South Dakota State University. I competed in two local events before qualifying for the Miss South Dakota pageant that year. My goal at that time was not necessarily to win the title, but to learn more about the job, as well as about myself, and make the top eight. I was not a finalist but I did accomplish the other two goals I had set. I was pleased.

The following year I qualified again for the Miss South Dakota pageant, with only one goal — to make the top eight. I did not succeed and as far as I was concerned, I was a failure. When in reality, by trying again, I had become a stronger person and a better performer.

My third try for the Miss South Dakota crown was much more successful. I performed a piano piece I wanted to play — not one that someone else told me the audience and the judges would like. I was second runner up, because I knew who I was and I listened to myself.

On my fourth try, I convinced myself that since there were many new girls in the pageant who had never competed before, and I had been second runner-up the previous year, I would not have to work as hard. Wrong! I did not win, learning all about the fallacy of being overconfident.

After that experience, I was through competing. Maybe God was telling me to quit. I already had a career and took losing as a sign to let go of the pageant part of my life. But when I called a friend the next day and told her about giving in, she said to me, "I am tired of people telling me that when an obstacle gets in their way, it's His way of telling you to give up. I believe it's actually God's way of testing you to make sure that it's something you truly want, and to which you give your all. God does not hand us our dreams like candy; we have to work for them.

After our conversation, I decided she was right, and competed in the last local of the year, paving the way for me to return to the Miss South Dakota pageant. Two weeks before I was to leave for the pageant, I called some friends. We got together and played football. We were just tossing the ball around on a nice summer day, something I had done many times before, but on one pass to me I caught the ball the wrong way and broke the ring finger on my left hand. The doctor told me that I had to have surgery and there was no way I could play the piano in two weeks. But I could not stop now. I went home, sat down at the piano and realized that I could relearn the fingering in my left hand, and I would be on the Miss South Dakota stage performing.

I put aside my goal to be Miss South Dakota 2001. Instead I was satisfied to be at the pageant making music on the piano. I was so relaxed that whole week, not trying to impress anyone, that I enjoyed myself more than ever before. The judges told me that is exactly why I won. They could see that I was genuine, not trying to be somebody I was not.

I learned that you do not give up when you get down, because you never know what you could have been if you do not keep trying.

My lesson on perseverance did not end when I won the Miss South Dakota crown. It was just the beginning after the tragic events of September 11.

I started thinking about how this was going to affect my year of service, and how I needed to present the role of Miss South Dakota. I realized that the people I represented of the Dignity and Respect for Seniors program would bring me in contact with the residents of nursing homes and assisted living centers. These people know what it means to persevere. Many of them had triumphed over difficult times in their lives; some have lived and fought in wars which we were so sure we would never have to experience.

As Miss South Dakota, I have tried to carry their messages of perseverance and courage, to respect their dignity and honor their memories. When I spoke to the young people in the schools. I encouraged them to rise to the challenge and emulate the courage of those who have won their battles in life.

As the journey of my Miss America competition comes to a close, I feel a deep sense of pride in the example we set — what it means to rise above adversity, and with a renewed sense of patriotism and pride in our country, serve our individual states bringing a message of hope and perseverance.

Miss Tennessee
2001

Stephanie
Culberson

The Gift of Giving

I grew up in a marvellous state that has a history of sons and daughters who are independent by nature. In school, long before a friend insisted I compete in a local beauty pageant, I learned that Spanish, French and English explorers and traders trailed through Tennessee in the sixteenth and seventeenth centuries hunting, trapping and looking for free land on which to build.

After the French and Indian Wars, "long hunters" from North Carolina and Virginia drifted into our valleys and hills and the Great Smokey Mountains and settled. One of them was Daniel Boone. Just as famous were Davy Crocket, Sam Houston and Andrew Jackson.

Why should I risk burdening you with some of the history of the state I love? The answer is that I strongly believe that the ideals these pioneers stood for are reflected in the modern citizens of the "volunteer state" and that makes me proud to be one of them.

I didn't make the connection of volunteerism, which was my platform as Miss Tennessee, with our state's motto until later.

Then, when I realized the coincidence, I was pleased that it happened. Tennessee became known as the Volunteer State, because in our war of 1812 with England, thousands of our young men volunteered for the army and distinguished themselves by their valor and bravery.

I grew up in Knoxville. Visitors to our mountainous area can get in touch with our antebellum past by visiting the Confederate memorial Hall here that served as Confederate headquarters during the Civil War siege of 1863.

A friend of mine convinced me to enter the local Cleveland, Tennessee beauty pageant. For a girl who never participated in contests, whose standard uniform was jeans, a shirt and a ball cap, the idea that I might win never entered my mind. I was too busy studying, playing the piano and working at part time jobs. My family isn't poor, but with three children, the idea that I might be eligible for scholarships was attractive. When I discovered that in one part of the competition I had to wear an evening dress, I was surprised. I didn't have one.

I was even more surprised when I learned I had won the Cleveland competition. When I didn't win a larger pageant which was a preliminary to the Miss Tennessee event, I was certain that this was the end of my competition experience.

The winner of Miss Tennessee was announced and my name was called. I was thunderstruck. How could this be happening to a girl who was happy as a tomboy, played football, climbed trees and did other *ungirlish* things?

But I did fall into the spirit of competition with 50 other young women in Atlantic City for a crown that would signify the wearer was much more than a pretty, talented girl. It was a symbol not only of the traditional Miss America gathering, but of the ceremony to honor and celebrate fifty-one of her daughters who represent the character, the strength and the achievement and dreams of every woman in the United States.

I thought about this after all of us went through the shock, slow recovery and emerging determination that we would not be cowed by a vicious attack on America. An attack that was meant to demonstrate the hate for us by fanatics so frightened by the idea of individual freedom of choice, of self determination by women, as well as men, that they would destroy it, to keep intact a culture of mental and religious confinement.

When it was time for us to vote on continuing with the pageant, I admit I was one of the minority to say No. It was later that I overcame my earlier conviction that compared with the attack on my country, the Miss America pageant was unimportant and should be cancelled. It came to me afterwards that we dare not delay the ceremony of a revered American institution. In doing so, we would become an ally in our own humiliation. That can never be.

Back home, I became engaged in the Miss Tennessee campaign to make our state drug free for school kids. I was Governor Don Sundquist's official spokesperson and I traveled 50,000 miles during my year of activity.

I cannot forget all the school boys and girls who welcomed me so warmly and took my message to heart about staying free of drugs. There were many serious moments as well as glad ones. One dear to my memory is the little boy who raised his hand in answer to my question, "Tell me what you want to be?"

He smiled, "When I grow up I want to be your husband."

A girl of fourteen who was recovering from drug addiction confessed to me, "I was afraid I might start using again until I heard you say that we can be anything we want to be. It gave me the courage to stay drug-free."

In particular, the kids responded to a quotation I recited to them from a Dr. Seuss book, *Oh, the Places You Go:*

> *You have brains in your head,*
> *And feet in your shoes.*
> *And you can steer yourself*
> *In any direction you chose.*

I believe that sums up the value I received from my year as Miss Tennessee and the lesson I learned from having had the opportunity of taking part in the Miss America 2001 pageant.

The tradition lives on, and I am proud of it all.

Miss Texas
2001

Stacy James

The Heart Goes On

W hen I first became aware of what had happened on the morning of September 11, my immediate thought was family. Quite honestly, I wanted to go home and be with my parents. All of a sudden, pageants lost their importance, and I had no desire to be in a competitive setting. As I prayed with the other girls on what to do, I began to realize, that while preparing a response to terrorism, America would not be cowed and would pursue its arts and culture. The pageant would go on. I have always tried to prioritize my life, with God being first, family second, and my particular job at the time third. That job was not only representing a state I love so much, but a country I love even more.

After the decision was made to move ahead, the contestants acknowledged that the competitive nature of a pageant was still prevalent, but more importantly all of us together represented the United States of America. I will never forget the bond that developed between us all, a wall of determination never to give in.

We could see the smoke pouring into the sky over New York. We were all horrified when one of the hostesses helping to make the week so special for us all left crying, because she had been notified that one of her relatives, (a cousin, I believe) was a pilot on the second plane that crashed into the World Trade Center.

My reign as Miss Texas started almost immediately after Miss America ended. I was asked to be at a black tie event hosted by John O'Hurley, who appeared on the Seinfeld series, the purpose of which was to raise money for Alzheimer's Disease, my platform. From that night on I suppose I have made over 350 appearances. I have talked to more than 100,000 public school-age children in the State of Texas (K through 12) where I have emphasized my particular program for Texas Cares for Children (something the Miss Texas Organization has been doing for a number of years) and the definition of what constitutes a quality life.

I have sung the national anthem and *America the Beautiful* at NASCAR Races, Texas Ranger and Houston Astro baseball games, and had the privilege recently of singing *My Heart Will Go On* at the National Alzheimer's Forum in Washington D.C. at the Lincoln Memorial. I do not think at any appearance, no matter what its purpose, have the events of the attack on America not been relevant or mentioned.

I remember looking at the words to *America the Beautiful* prior to the NASCAR Race and noticing, as though for the first time, that as an American, I was not as familiar with the second verse as I should have been. From students throughout my state, from all ethnic backgrounds, I could not have missed the renewal in love of country and love of freedom. It is not put on, but very real. Like me, individuals who have never known war are more appreciative now than ever of the sacrifices that must be made in order to preserve our way of life.

Although my ultimate strength is my faith in God, I have been strengthened by the young people I have met throughout Texas who I know as adults will typify the character and fortitude needed to preserve the freedom that is unique to the United States.

As my reign now ends, I often look at the videotapes of the various experiences I have had as Miss Texas. These acts of reminiscence are not from ego, but rather from pride, and the Lord leads me, to remind myself of all that has happened to me over the past year. As I do that, I often reflect on that day of terror in September and my week with 50 other wonderful human beings yearning to be Miss America. This is especially true of the videotape of the Forum in Washington D.C. on Alzheimer's. I remember the many delegates who were there from all over the nation as they held their lighted candles facing the Lincoln Memorial with the water from the Washington Monument glittering behind them. The song I sang from the movie *Titanic, My Heart Will Go On,* was most appropriate for those of us who have lost loved ones to Alzheimer's Disease.

The heart does go on and never really forgets a loved one who has made a major impact on one's life. However, the song was also appropriate to celebrate the resolve that rose from the terror of 9/11. If I live to be 100, the events of that day will never dim in my mind. As I think of all the brave men and women in our country, especially in New York, who responded to the tragedy, the patriotic and heartfelt love I have for the United States of America will go on forever.

Miss Utah 2001

Jaclyn Hunt

The Flame of Patriotism

*A*s I woke up on that September 11 morning in my room at Caesar's Palace in Atlantic City, I was looking straight into the sun rising on the Atlantic Ocean. I didn't think for a second that there could be a more perfect day. I would go to the gym, practice the piano. and return to my room to watch the news on CNN and getting ready for my interview. About a half hour later, my travel companion, Viola, and I watched the breaking news, and learned that "something" terrible was happening at New York City's World Trade Center. We were aghast to see a second plane hit the other tower while the first one started to come tumbling down. I called my family to let them know that I was all right, and we were leaving for rehearsals.

There, all of us sat in the dressing room, huddled around a small radio listening to the news of what was happening to two of America's great landmarks. It was also frightening for me to realize that we, the contestants for Miss America, were a living landmark and icon of America. Someone suggested that we pray and we all held hands while a prayer was offered. Suddenly it didn't matter that we were all of different religions and that God was the only one who could help us or give us comfort.

As the day wore on, we were sent to our hotels. I watched the news for a long time, wrote of my experiences that day in my journal, turned off the light and tried to sleep. I laid there thinking about how changed the world would be when I woke up, and what could happen while I slept. I even questioned whether or not I would wake up. I was twenty years old and didn't dare sleep in my hotel room by myself. I didn't want to wake Viola in her room, so I turned the light back on to read from my journal about the time when I received a blessing from my priest and from John Groberg, a general authority from my church.

Instead of blessing me with grace, beauty, and poise, these men had blessed me with safety and protection as I spent my days at the Miss America Pageant. Suddenly, it all made sense. They did not know what our country would be facing during the time I was in Atlantic City, but a loving Heavenly Father knew, and He knew how I would be feeling while I was alone in that hotel room. He had inspired my church leaders to assure me that I would be safe and protected. As I read that, I knew that there was no reason for me to fear and that everything would be all right.

At a time when it seemed as if the world was blaming God for not preventing this tragedy, I was thanking Him for the peace He had sent me just days before the attacks.

Later, when we were called upon to vote as to whether or not to continue with the pageant my feelings were mixed. I didn't know if we could get up on stage, smile, and compete for the title of Miss America when the whole country was in mourning. Yet as I thought of how President Bush and Mayor Giuliani and even Utah's Governor Leavitt were encouraging us to move forward with life, I realized that this was a time for Miss America, that a new Miss America would be someone who could uplift our spirits and help our nation to begin the healing process.

My favorite moment at Miss America was not making the top ten or winning the Quality of Life Award, it was our candlelight vigil on September 14th. I was at the very top of the stairs so I could see as the flame was passed from girl to girl, from state to state, all the way up. It was so awesome for me to realize that at that time our whole nation was participating in this ritual and here we were the torchbearers from every state coming together to say that we love and support America. At that moment a surge of patriotism flooded me with a passion I had never before experienced.

I have shared my September 11, almost daily with every audience I have spoken to as Miss Utah. Freedom, patriotism, and the love of God have come to mean so much more in my life. When I returned home to Utah I made an arrangement of patriotic music for the piano, and played at almost every appearance after sharing my experiences during the attacks.

The events of September 11 reaffirmed my year as Miss Utah in almost every way. Because of the freedoms my country has given me, I can wear makeup, evening gowns, swimsuits, speak to large audiences, and pursue a higher education. I am more grateful for my family and friends. I am kinder in relationships with others. I realize how precious life is. I am less superficial and more forgiving.

I am so proud to be an American.

Miss Vermont 2001

Amy Marie Johnson

Vital Signs

*L*ast September, I had the honor of representing the Green Mountain State of Vermont at the Miss America Pageant in Atlantic City. It was the culmination of a dream that began when I dressed up as Miss America for Halloween when I was four years old.

In the days that followed the tragedy in New York, I maintained some kind of normality by running on the treadmill and following CNN. When the names of the victims of United Flight 173 traveling from Boston to Los Angeles flashed on the screen, I was stunned, for I saw my college friend and co-worker, Lisa Frost, 21, from Santa Clara, California flash on the screen. I couldn't believe it. She was a young woman, newly graduated from college with honors, who was headed back to Los Angeles to begin her first job. Four months earlier I presented her with our college's top community service award. Lisa was young with such a good heart: I was sure she would make a difference in the world. Now her life had ended.

My next few days were spent with the other Miss America contestants, praying, watching the news, consoling each other, and trying to decide if we wanted to go on with the Miss America Pageant. Total negativity invaded my own personal thoughts: thoughts which focused on a desire to go home and be with my family. So many lost loved ones, and so many lives had changed.

Here I was in Atlantic City trying to prepare myself to compete in swimsuit and talent. I wondered, "How is this relevant?" Thursday was to be the day that the 51 contestants would vote to decide what to do. The two choices were: a) change the mood of the pageant to be more patriotic, or b) not have the pageant or a Miss America 2001. Wednesday night I felt prepared and confident with my vote not to have the pageant. The night before our vote to continue or discontinue I couldn't justify prancing around in my evening gown while there was so much devastation and pain in our country and world.

I went to sleep with those thoughts; but when I woke up on Thursday morning I had changed my mind. I had dreamed about the Miss America pageant, seeing myself competing in talent, performing my piano solo, and standing proudly onstage to take my bow. I saw myself walking down the runway, smiling to Lisa, my friend who had lost her life as her plane hit the second tower of our World Trade Center. She was seated in the front row in Atlantic City waving an American Flag.

Generally, I view my dreams as small random events and pieces from the previous day muddled together as one. This dream was different. It seemed to me that it was my symbol to continue on with the competition. It was the right thing to do. Then, I realized that Miss America is a tradition in this country. She is a role model and an icon of hope and patriotism. This year's Miss America would be an emblem of courage, a statement that our country cannot be defeated or demoralized. I felt I was at the Miss America Pageant for a reason, and no one should ever be allowed to stop our traditions. No one can shatter the spirit of our nation.

When I returned from Atlantic City, I decided to be as visible as possible in my travels around the state and mirror the courage of all Americans. I cannot forget how endearing so many of my more than 200 appearances have been. There was a little girl's father, who called my mother in complete desperation because his son had drawn a mustache on the autographed picture I had given his daughter at school.

Or the little girl who put her arms around my legs, looked up at me and said, "I want to be just like you when I grow up." Memories like these have helped me to realize the magnitude of winning the Miss Vermont title. Along with its many prizes came the job of teaching children to reach for the stars; teaching them that anything they want to do is achievable. That message is important for children of all ages. It's even more vital today because of the anxiety September 11 brought to us.

The title of Miss Vermont gave me the opportunity and the megaphone that I needed to spread this message.

Miss Virginia 2001

Meghan Shanley

It's all About Service

*W*hen I was crowned Miss Virginia in June of 2001, my first thought when they called my name was, "What have I done?" I really wasn't sure if I could handle the great responsibility that came with a title of this magnitude, but I remembered that God never gives us more than we can handle. There was never a greater need to remember this than on September 11, 2001. That morning, after we all learned of the day's events, we congregated in the grand ballroom of the convention center. Huddled around a black and white eight inch television, we could do nothing but stay glued to the screen for any new information.

My journal entry for that evening gives my personal insight into what was going through our minds.

"Today is the saddest and most unbelievable day in American history. This morning around 8:45, a hijacked plane flew or crashed into one of the Twin Towers of the World Trade Center in New York City. Twenty-one minutes later a second plane crashed into the second of the towers, and eventually they both collapsed. About 40,000 people are estimated to work in these buildings. The number of casualties is unknown because the buildings are still too unsafe to go near. Within an hour of the New York crashes, another hijacked plane crashed into the Pentagon in Washington D.C. A fourth plane crashed in a rural area in Pennsylvania. Four planes and thousands of lives have been lost today. They are saying that this makes the attack on Pearl Harbor look miniscule.

No one knows just how many people have been lost. Here in the midst of a national tradition, Miss America, we are at a loss to know what is going on. They are considering postponing the pageant and we may also be threatened, since American traditions and icons are being targeted. Security is so hyped up. There are bomb sniffing dogs everywhere. We got to the convention center already shaken this morning and after we had finally started to calm down we heard blood curdling screams and learned that someone had just received a phone call notification that a relative had gone down on the Pennsylvania plane. Her screams struck my soul like nothing ever has. Never have I heard sounds like those before. They moved us out of that room and sent dogs through the rest of the building to secure the areas. They cancelled all of our events for the day and frankly are not sure if we are even going to have a pageant. Today all of the airspace over the nation has been shut down.

"I'm writing in this journal as I watch the non-stop footage of today's events. One tape includes views of people jumping from unbelievable heights to escape a fiery, yet inescapable death. Another shows the second plane crashing right into the tower. It's estimated that more than 200 New York police and firemen are dead after the buildings eventually collapsed. I really need to get some sleep, my eyes are stinging from crying.

"We don't know what we'll be doing tomorrow. This puts life in a new perspective. I really thought this would be an amazing week, and that the Miss America event would be the greatest time-of-my-life experience. But the pageant has diminished in importance when I think about how many lives were shattered by today's tragedy. I cherish my family more every hour. There is nowhere to turn but to God. He holds our future in His hands. He is the only one who can ease our pain. That knowing is the only calming thought in a day that has been so laden with evil, chaos and destruction."

Finally we came to the conclusion that indeed the pageant would go on, to show the strength of America. That attitude was the beginning of a theme for my year of service. The great opportunity to use my title to significantly influence people's lives was a constant in my mind from that point on.

Many people think of the Miss America Pageant as a dream come true for so many little girls. It is indeed that, but if utilized properly, the title for a young woman representing a state is an opportunity for her to be a servant to her community. The prestige that comes with the crown can be so powerful. A perfect example is when an eighty-year-old veteran with tears in his eyes, said to me, "I never thought I'd see the day when I'd meet Miss Virginia."

However, I was the one in awe of him, because of his lifelong service to our country. Having been raised in a Navy family I have always respected the many sacrifices that men and women make for our country everyday. This year gave me a chance to voice that gratitude to all whom I addressed. I have hosted the USO Holiday Show at the Norfolk Naval Station for four years now. This show is taped and sent out to all who are at sea during the holidays.

It was very difficult this year trying to film an inspiring and uplifting show while knowing we were at war with an unknown enemy. I was able to share my love of singing with members of the military and their families. I recorded a special message that was sent out to each ship. It was a chance for me to assist in providing a little bit of happiness to those who continue to give so much to us.

During my year of service, I had two appearances alongside New York firefighters who were there on September 11. It was a chance to hear firsthand descriptions of the day that so many speak of, but so few have an actual mental grasp of. A large concern of mine has been that young people do not show enough gratitude to these well deserving heroes.

Throughout the year, on some of my days off, I made trips to local fire stations and military bases to personally thank the fire-fighters and military personnel. Later in the year, during an appearance at an elementary school, I had quite a heart warming experience.

At the end of my presentation I announced that the song I was going to sing was one they all knew, and to feel free to sing along. As I began to sing *God Bless America,* the room filled with the voices of these children singing at the top of their lungs. I always invite audiences to sing along to this song, but never had I gotten such an overwhelming reaction, especially with elementary school students. I heard the pride in their voices for singing this song, and it alleviated some of the concern I'd had earlier.

This year has been such a blessing and was possible only in one way as set out in Philippians 4:13, "I can do all things through Christ who strengthens me." That strength united every one of the 51 young women who were part of the Miss America experience.

Miss Washington 2001

Breann Parriott

The Human Touch

A tangible current of excitement crackled through the crowded dressing room as the first 16 of the 51 Miss America 2001 contestants arrived for the beginning day of rehearsal at historic Convention Hall on the Atlantic City Boardwalk. Many of us had dreamed of this day from the time we were children. We were sharing the same dressing room and the same traditions as decades of state titleholders had done before us. This would be an unforgettable day.

Amid the high timbre of eager voices and bursts of laughter, I caught a glimpse of a female security guard entering a side door and approaching the dressing room chaperone, who was grinning broadly while observing our excitement as we laid out clothes, make up, water bottles, and hair brushes. The guard whispered something to her, and the smile dropped from her face as though she had seen a ghost.

I knew something was not right. As she called for our attention, the pace in the dressing room slowed moderately to acknowledge what we anticipated would be a brief announcement. I remember her mouth forming the words: "It appears New York City is under terrorist attack." My mind did not grasp the meaning. The dressing room fell into silence. No one moved. Miss Alaska, Eugenia Primis gasped, her brother worked in downtown Manhattan. Gradually, the news penetrated my consciousness, and shock and disbelief ran through me. Miss Colorado grabbed her mini boom box she'd brought to play her talent music for rehearsing, and frantically searched for a wall plug.

En masse, we gathered around her, and I saw my own concern and confusion mirrored on the faces of my Miss America sisters. Confined to the hollow depths of Convention Hall, we had no access to television, and the small radio sputtered only static as we stood in frustrated silence. Finally a voice came across the air waves, "A jet liner has crashed into one of the World Trade Center Towers in New York City. The number of casualties is yet unknown, but the loss of life is devastating. We do not yet know the reason for the crash."

Emotions came unleashed in the previously quiet dressing room. Our only response was to reach out for one another, for the comfort of a hand, a hug, a shoulder. We huddled together around the small radio and listened helplessly as the events unfolded and the radio announcer drew word pictures for us of the devastation and death as the tower collapsed, and a second airplane crashed into the other tower of the tall World Trade Center. Next we heard that the Pentagon was hit, the second tower collapsed, and another plane downed in Philadelphia, where we had just spent a beautifully hosted weekend.

Soon the rest of the contestants began to arrive in shifts, unloading into the dressing room with tear-stained faces, and rushing to the comfort of our small, desperate huddle, which seemed to offer some sense of unity and safety.

There in the dressing room at the Miss America Pageant, our nation represented by one delegate from each state and the District of Columbia, we united. As a group we cried for our country, we mourned for those who paid the terrorists' ransom with their lives, we lamented and grieved at the blatant attack on freedom, and then on our knees we fought back with the power of prayer. One trembling hand reached for the one beside hers, and a strong circle formed as all 51 women joined a seamless chain to stand for their states and their nation.

As I look back on that day and the following weeks, my strongest response to the events of September 11 remains focused on the strength we found in reaching out for each other. We sought comfort and solace not by standing alone, but from standing together. The touch of another person brought some momentary relief and a promise that together we would get through it all.

More than any other lesson I learned during my year of service, I became aware of the power of touch, and the need to feel connected to one another. The connection to another human being conveyed through touch occurs not by accident, but yet so often goes unnoticed. We express concern, love, anger, and curiosity in the way we connect physically with one another. In the wake of the tragedy our nation endured in the Fall of 2001, the life lesson I have taken with me is the knowledge that the quality of a handshake, the length of a hug, and the meaning expressed in touch should not be taken for granted.

As a nation, we need to take the time to reach out to each other more often and realize that unity is not found in independence, but rather in interdependence. It is my desire to encourage you to take the time to reach out to those around you, and take special care in the manner of your interaction with your business acquaintances, your family and friends.

Pause over a handshake, extend the length of a hug, linger over a kiss, offer a hand to help and don't be afraid of the comfort and strength found in a touch. I thank you, Miss America Class of 2001, for teaching me the value of reaching out to the person next to you.

United We Stand.

Miss Washington D.C. 2001

Marshawn Evans

Survive: For Such a Time as This

*I*t was the first day of rehearsals in Atlantic City for the 2001 Miss America competition. "Am I really here?" I thought. "Could I truly be a part of this rich American tradition?" I answered a proud yet humble, "Yes" to myself as I prepared to go downstairs for my early morning workout. It was an interesting morning, and I knew it would be a challenging day. As I reflected on the opportunity I now possessed, I became so proud to represent the nation's capitol … Washington D.C. As a young girl growing up in the south, I experienced as many obstacles as I did opportunities. I knew that there were a number of people who would probably be very surprised to see me the following week as I competed on national television for the title of Miss America. As I continued my workout, I thought about the elementary school I had attended and the teachers who sought to make me feel inferior. They almost succeeded, but, thankfully, I learned to turn that negative energy into my motivation to excel. That trying period during my childhood even motivated me through that soon-to-be infamous morning as I finished my last set of push-ups.

I jumped in the shower to get ready for rehearsals. I eagerly anticipated learning the production numbers and beginning competition. I always believed that all of my experiences — good and bad — as a child, teenager, and now as a young adult were preparing me for such a time as this. Five minutes later, I discovered how one of the biggest tests of time would manifest itself in my life. My traveling companion rapped urgently on the door and told me that an accident had happened in New York — that a plane had lost control and accidentally crashed into one of the World Trade Center Towers. My experiences and feelings of shock, disbelief, and uncertainty over the next 30–45 minutes paralleled that of most Americans on the morning of September 11. We were clearly being attacked and no one knew if their safety was guaranteed anywhere in America. Both Twin Towers were struck. I was concerned about the people there as well as my family. And, then, a plane crashed into the Pentagon not five miles from where I live outside of Washington D.C. The news of the attack on our capitol overwhelmed me. I had just been there a few months earlier for a tour. I drove by the Pentagon regularly.

Living near the monuments and historic buildings in Washington D.C. made it impossible for me to imagine anyone of them not being there, or being destroyed. Our capitol represents the strength and fortitude that makes America the most admired country in the world. Now Washington D.C., was being viciously attacked.

I thought about my friends who worked in the District and at the Pentagon. I thought about all the children from schools around the country who were visiting our capitol that day. I called my dad, an air traffic controller, who was not working that day. He could not explain to me how a hijacking could take place in America in the year 2001. It was at that point that I became nervous. Dad always had the answers.

Then, I called my roommate. She told me that everything was alright in our neighborhood. She, like most of my friends, was shaken up, and told me that her sister was on the freeway adjacent to the Pentagon, and watched as the plane crashed into the building.

Just as the realization of what had actually happened in my backyard began to sink in, I heard another tap on the door. It was time to go to rehearsals.

"Rehearsals?" I asked. I guess I was right. This was going to be an interesting and challenging day. When I saw the other 50 young women at the convention center, I immediately noticed that we all had one thing in common. The look in everyone's eyes — one that I can hardly describe — reflected the uncertainties we were all experiencing. Four days earlier, I met the same group of 50 women that I believed to be among the most tenacious, caring, and awe inspiring in America. Now, they were different. With all my heart, I firmly believe we drew upon each others' inner resources, and together we channeled them into fearless determination.

Deciding to go forward with the competition was difficult. I went to Atlantic City to compete for the title of Miss America so that I could have the opportunity to inspire people and fulfill my life's mission statement, "To enrich lives, build communities and strengthen the future." My purpose in pursuing the crown was far bigger than myself. I had accepted a responsibility to represent Washington D.C and its spirit of hope, focus, faith and freedom. Our nation has never quit. Neither have I. Hardship and trials of the past had prepared me for such a time as this, and it was time to go forward.

The next several days were filled with prayer and focus. I did not know what the future would hold, but I knew who held my future. I continually drew strength from seeing the depth of America's resilience. How proud I was to live in the land of the free and the home of the brave. Once the competition began, maintaining a sense of focus seemed impossible, but was certainly imperative. After winning the interview phase the first night, and then the talent portion of the competition in my group the second night, a variety of feelings swept over me. I had worked hard and was overjoyed, yet still saddened by the sorrow that surrounded us all. I prayed for purpose. All things work for the good for those who love God. I knew I was here for such a time as this.

On the final night of competition, a remarkable sense of peace settled over me. I was honored to be called to the top five and the chance to perform my talent. A baton twirling routine to *I Will*

Survive. This had been the theme song for my life. Teachers labeled me an incapable problem child. Instead, I became a Truman scholar and was accepted to law school. Doctors told me I could not twirl because I was legally blind in my left eye, yet two nights ago, I won the talent competition at Miss America. Now, it was my time to share my story of inspiration and hope with America.

Ten days after September 11, I performed on national television in front of 15 million people to my theme song *I Will Survive* to let everyone know that we would not crumble, we would not lay down and die.

I will never forget the overwhelming sight of the Pentagon with the black, charred hole in its side that represented the darkness and evil of a cowardly attack. Even then, I became hopeful. It is during times of struggle, not success, when a nation reveals its true character. America is a resilient country full of determination and hope, and a country committed to facing hardship head on. On September 11, we learned that problems, challenges, adversity, and obstacles are inevitable.

Living life, however, is not about how many trials you face. It is about how you handle them, and the message you send in the midst of adversity. I learned early on that the past should be used as a springboard, not a hammock. Life is about turning obstacles into opportunities, challenges into chances, and problems into purposeful possibilities. In essence, life is about overcoming and having the determination to survive. We will survive.

Miss West Virginia 2001

Danaé DeMasi

From Rhinestones to Reality

*I*n the fall of 1988 I watched Kay Lani Rae Rafko of Michigan become the new Miss America, and on a late night of June 23rd, 2001, I was astonished to find out that I was going to walk that very same stage. My dream as a child of fulfilling the legend of Miss America was finally becoming tangible. I was crowned Miss West Virginia and was on my way to represent our beautiful Mountain State in Atlantic City!

As a girl I thought that Miss America was the most beautiful woman in the world. It wasn't until years later that I realized Miss America was chosen for her inner beauty, intellectual beauty, and the strength she possessed to make a positive change in the world around her. Those attributes were in demand on September 11, 2001.

I will always remember that day as the one that changed rhinestones to reality. I was sitting watching the news with the other contestants in the rehearsal room. Every girl there had dreamed like I of becoming Miss America, and now it seemed to me it didn't matter at all who won — being Miss America seemed almost silly. I was actually a bit embarrassed.

During the next few days those feelings of embarrassment turned to fear, then just plain anger. How dare someone attack the place I call home, and jeopardize the freedom I have as an American citizen? I feel so lucky to have had each and every single one of those 50 other contestants to talk to during those difficult next few days. We discussed opinions and feelings as well as our new perceptions of our jobs as Miss America state titleholders. As the days passed I started to feel better about being in Atlantic City and I realized that my childhood dream was not as frivolous as I first thought.

On September 11, 2001, I learned if nothing else that every life has a purpose. During my time in Atlantic City, I also learned that we needed a Miss America to represent our values and act as a role model to promote them. We decided with much thought to go ahead with the pageant. I figured that if I was not chosen as Miss America, I owed it to the youth of West Virginia to be the best moti-vational speaker, and the most effective Miss West Virginia. Our youth needs to know that they are valued for their vision, and for their voices, and that it is up to them to use those tools wisely by making good decisions.

Although I was pleased with my top ten finish, I was not named Miss America 2002. I also learned that being Miss America was not in my life path. Instead, it was meant for me to travel around and rally my state on what it feels like to be an American. I live my platform speaking on literacy and education. Education is something that no one can take away from you. West Virginians may not live life in the fast lane, but in our state we have a sense of community, family, and religion which I love to promote.

Almost every morning my alarm goes off early, and I awake disoriented until I realize that I am in a hotel room and not in the comfort of my nice soft bed at home. I eat breakfast, quickly get dressed in one of my favorite suits, jump in the car, check my map as I travel from town to town on some often remote country roads. When I arrive at my destination, I don a microphone pack, and turn to face an audience of 100 to 500 students at any given time. I'm not a beauty queen — I am a motivational speaker, and as Miss

West Virginia, I am able to carry my message on issues that are important to me.

I make sure that I tell the students about my perspective on the 9/11 tragedy, and how important it is to receive a good education, make good decisions, and to never give up your dreams. This year I have received $21,000 in scholarship money, went on a 55-county tour across the state of West Virginia, and had the chance of a lifetime to influence the lives of others.

Being Miss West Virginia enabled me to earn my master's degree, and confirm that I am smart enough and strong enough to take care of myself. I can depend on me to get what I want out of life. This is one of the best feelings in the world.

This past September my priorities in life were changed. I make sure that I take nothing for granted, especially this opportunity of a lifetime to be a positive role model for our youth. That is a job I take seriously. Always remember that you don't need a shiny crown to make good decisions or be a good role model, for someday you too might find yourself going from rhinestones to reality.

Miss Wisconsin 2001

Laura Margaret Herriot

We Are Americans

*L*ast September, fifty-one excited Miss America contestants clambered aboard the train in Philadelphia for our trip to Atlantic City. An event we were all experiencing for the first time. As we approached Atlantic City, attitudes changed. While we were still the connected group of women that had arrived in Philadelphia a few days earlier, our attitudes had changed and toughened. Some were determined to walk home with the Miss America crown; others sought media exposure; some were grateful and proud to have been chosen from thousands of young women to represent the best of America. I was there for the experience. I knew it could never happen to me again; and the opportunities to speak to my country about organ and tissue donation awareness was unlimited. Little did I realize that the next morning my job as Miss Wisconsin was about to change drastically.

On September 11 I awoke in "pageant" mode, focused on beginning rehearsals on the day that would shock the world. I was in the general dressing room sitting at my assigned station with several other girls, when a female officer rushed in to tell us that a jet plane had struck one of the Twin Towers of the World Trade Center in New York City. The screaming, yelling and the visible shock of the contestants and volunteers confused me, and I didn't understand what had happened. Moments later, I learned that another plane had struck the other Twin Tower. A newscaster called it a terrorist attack.

Immediately, the Miss America pageant no longer seemed important. I sat there staring at myself in the mirror and lowered my head. I prayed to God to help those in New York, and to protect my family and friends and my new pageant sisters. And at that moment of awe, anger and grief, I could see the gathering of unity among the women from fifty-one different parts of the United States. It was impressive, and I felt honored to be part of such an unselfish group — and even more so, when we later voted to keep the pageant going.

When I returned home to Wisconsin, I saw immediately what an impact 9/11 had made on everyday lives. American flags flew high everywhere. People eagerly donated their time and efforts to show New Yorkers they were not alone. We were going to fight this as one.

As Miss Wisconsin, my prior focus had been solely on organ and tissue donation, but I came to realize quickly that it was proper for me to reference how the victims of the attack never had the opportunity to be an organ or tissue donor. Many of the families of the lost never had the chance to say goodbye or to reassure their loved one's spirits because they were taken so quickly. Parades took on a different meaning, for they reminded spectators of their stake in the American Flag. Marching citizens expressed the hope and vitality of our nation.

One of my final appearances as Miss Wisconsin was to perform as a soloist an original version of *God Bless America* with a back-up choir in Waubeka, Wisconsin — home of the American Flag. This was not only the location where our flag was declared our national symbol, but it was the home from which my heritage sprung. It was a moving day, and I was grateful that my entire family was able to be there for this event.

My grandfather was a World War II veteran and during the Flag Day celebration, he and I toured the Flag Day museum. Inside, he saw a replica of the uniform he wore during his war time service. He was surprised and proud when he noticed the name on the lapel of the uniform was his own. I realized then, that my role as Miss Wisconsin was so much more than just a title; it has been a rebuilding experience for my family, for my community and for our nation.

We have given hope in the face of a storm.

We have risen above the challenge.

And we have shown courage that cannot be shaken.

We Are Americans!

Miss Wyoming 2001

Erin Empey

Knowing the Difference

*A*mong our friends and many of the theatre patrons of Casper, Wyoming, our family is characterized as dramatic and eccentric. The new buzzword "drama" used to describe issues, problems or events full of turmoil or happiness, is in fact my favorite word because it vividly describes my life, the people around me, and the events in which I am involved. The night I won the title of Miss Wyoming, June 2nd, 2001, that characterization became true once again. And humorously this time. As my name was announced as the new state title-holder, my father bowed his head in his hands in annoyance and disbelief, a reaction that summarized my father's artistic temperament. My mother, a dedicated supporter of her children, shouted at the top of her lungs so the entire audience would know: "That's my Baby!"

My reaction, however, was a mixture of both their attitudes, as any child's would be. The first words out of my mouth after being crowned was, "What the h--- am I doing?" This comment, along with the surprised reaction of my parents came to summarize my year as Miss Wyoming.

I had always been apprehensive of the title Miss Wyoming because I believed that no one living in Wyoming would know the difference between Miss Wyoming and Miss Rodeo Wyoming, who is associated with a frontier art so popular in our state. I am probably as far away from the typical Wyomingite as you can imagine. I prefer ballet and sushi to rodeo and steak. I attribute my interests to my parents, whose philosophy expresses the fact, that while we may live in a small town, we will never have small minds. Our family vacations consist of visiting museums and places of history rather than theme parks and Hawaii. It was always very important to my parents to have their children exposed to culture and diversity, and, most importantly, to try new things that would bring to them challenges and awareness. This personal desire of my parents to try new things became the sole influence for my decision to compete for the title of Miss Wyoming.

Pageants became a new addition to my life when I competed in my very first event, The Miss Wyoming Scholarship Pageant. It was in fact the scholarship money that persuaded me to participate as well as the recommendation from my parents to grab the opportunity of experiencing a whole new aspect of life. It was through the year of representing the state of Wyoming that I realized this program was about much more than just a scholarship award — it was about shaping young women into who they wish to be.

What an adventure my year would be. I had no concept of the opportunities it would hold for me, or the challenges, or even the blessings. I was naive in preparing for Miss America, my second pageant experience, and was frightened of the situations I might find myself in. Coming from a Western state that was not financially supportive and with a sparsely put-together Board of Directors, I knew honestly and realistically that Wyoming did not have much of a chance at winning the title of Miss America.

Therefore, I decided to set my goals for something more attainable. The most influential aspect of a positive experience, I concluded, would be for me to just be myself. That was a characteristic I had always been taught and it has especially been emphasized at this time when I needed guidance and comfort. I also knew it was the perspective that I would need to get through the unknown.

Unknown it was. Tuesday morning, September 11, left every young woman present at Miss America with strong uncertainty. Uncertainty of their safety, their security and their emotions. On the day after, the fifty-one contestants were confronted with the decision of whether or not to continue with the pageant. During the discussion that involved us all, we agreed that no matter what the decision was, we would support each other. I recognized later that this was the precise moment that our unique sisterhood became divided.

My reaction was a passionate No! I felt that it was our responsibility as representatives of each state to return home and comfort those who needed us and whom we needed. I believed then that it was irreverent and disrespectful to continue as scheduled. I have to admit, that in the two-to-one vote cast by the girls, I was part of the thirty-three percent minority who voted No. I wanted to see my parents leave the East Coast, which is far away from home, and to end an experience that was moving me out of my comfort zone.

What I believed to be a private vote became fodder for the newspapers as well as a test of my integrity. During my interview with the pageant judges I was asked what my vote had been. I had to decide if I had the strength to stand behind my conviction and admit that I had been in the minority, and I did. By the end of my Miss America experience I recognized how important it truly was to have carried through this adversity and tragic period of history. Because of what happened on September 11, our year would be like none other before. I also believe that opening each day with a prayer created the spiritual bond that still unites us, and helped special relationships to be nurtured and grow.

Back home, I traveled as Miss Wyoming, throughout my state speaking about my platform of the Arts in Education. I was repeatedly asked by students and administrators about my Miss America experience. I always reply that it was a life-changing experience, and I have never forgotten a quotation written on the wall of a middle school that summarized my feelings about my Miss America and Miss Wyoming experience:

> *"Don't cry that it's over,*
> *Smile because it happened."*

*If you are lucky enough to find a way of life
you love, you have to find the courage to live it.*

– John Irving

To order additional copies of

Under the Crown

Book: $14.95   Shipping/Handling: $5.00

Contact:

Hara Publishing
P.O. Box19732
Seattle, Washington 98109

800-461-1931